Twayne's English Authors Series

EDITOR OF THIS VOLUME

Sylvia E. Bowman

Indiana University

Oscar Wilde

TEAS 211

Oscar Wilde

OSCAR WILDE

By DONALD H. ERICKSEN
Illinois State University

TWAYNE PUBLISHERS
A DIVISION OF G. K. HALL & CO., BOSTON

Library of Congress Cataloging in Publication Data

Ericksen, Donald H
  Oscar Wilde.

  (Twayne's English authors series ; TEAS 211)
  Bibliography: p. 169–71.
  Includes index.
  1. Wilde, Oscar, 1854–1900—Criticism and
interpretation.
PR5824.E7   828'.8'09   77-22763
ISBN 0-8057-6680-4

MANUFACTURED IN THE UNITED STATES OF AMERICA

Contents

About the Author

Currently Professor of English at Illinois State University, Donald H. Ericksen has also taught at the Universities of Illinois and Arizona. He received his Bachelor of Arts from Valparaiso University, his Master of Arts from Northwestern University, and his Doctor of Philosophy degree from the University of Illinois with a dissertation on the critical history of the novels of Charles Dickens. Professor Ericksen's work on Charles Dickens, Charlotte Brontë, and other Victorian writers has appeared in a number of journals, among them the *Victorian Newsletter*, the *Arizona Quarterly*, and the *Journal of English and Germanic Philology*. Now, in addition to lecturing in Nineteenth and Twentieth Century British literature, he is working on a booklength study of Victorian art and fiction.

Preface

Oscar Wilde, the man, has always fascinated readers and critics no less than Oscar Wilde, the artist. But this double interest in both Wilde's personality and his work has also been one of the major sources of the persistent critical difficulties that have arisen both during his creative lifetime and the three quarters of a century since his death. Too often the artistic merits of individual works have been slighted in order to stress their significance as literary monuments of the Decadence. Criticism has been overly concerned with the light it might shed upon the mind and personality of Oscar Wilde while the more significant task—assessing the particular nature and qualities of Wilde's literary works—has been too often overlooked. The contrary tendency, the effort to shed new light on Wilde's literary achievement by studies of the artist's life and personality, has been similarly overdone. No doubt some of these critical problems have arisen because Oscar Wilde's personality and works both appear to have been shaped by the same artistic principles. When Wilde, the dandy, affirms the importance of living up to his blue china the comment is not inexplicable, but rather is Wilde's way of expressing the idea central to his artistic credo that "the critical and cultured spirits . . . will seek to gain their impressions almost entirely from what Art has touched. For Life is terribly deficient in form." Hence, it is the responsibility of such "critical and cultured" spirits to make their lives and personalities as much works of art as the poems and plays they admire or aspire to create.

A parallel weakness in a substantial number of the critical accounts of Wilde's life and art has been the tendency to see both Oscar Wilde and his works as historical and literary anomalies rather than products of the shaping influences of the nineteenth century. Too often Wilde is considered narrowly as an artist set apart, a creative spirit existing in a state of cultural hostility to a stuffy Victorian Age, an attitude Wilde himself encouraged in his writings, life, and letters. The Edwardian reaction to Aestheticism and all that it represented certainly perpetuated and encouraged this tendency. The truth, of course, is that Wilde is very much a part of his age. He is a literary and critical descendant of the Romantics, and the literary and critical ancestor of such leading figures of the twentieth century as William Butler Yeats, T.S. Eliot, Roland Barthes, and Northrop Frye.

In order to avoid the two critical tendencies mentioned above, I have placed my primary emphasis upon critical/analytical assessments of individual works. An effort has been made in the case of each work to shed some new light upon persistent and significant critical problems. An equally important effort has been made to point up the significant relationships that exist among Wilde's works, such as the relationships of the style and intellectual content of Wilde's short fiction to the artistic ideas of *Intentions*, his single volume of criticism published in 1891, or the connections between Wilde's critical theories and his obvious fascination in his drama and poetry with the figure of Christ. A consequence of this recognition of the myriad relationships among Wilde's poems, fiction, plays, and critical essays is a healthy awareness of the essential artistic unity of Wilde's creative output, a good grasp of the nature of his growth as a literary artist, and, finally, a powerful sense of the importance of Oscar Wilde's place in English literary history.

Because Wilde was an important poet, dramatist, novelist, critic, short story writer, journalist, lecturer, celebrity, editor, and wit, the necessity for placing some limits upon this study is clear. Almost all of Wilde's significant critical thought is contained in the four essays of *Intentions*, the "Soul of Man Under Socialism," and "The Portrait of Mr. W.H." Consideration of Wilde's critical thought, therefore, has been limited for the most part to these central works. I have devoted a chapter to his short fiction and children's stories for they represent a major portion of Wilde's achievement as a literary artist yet have been given little of the critical attention they deserve.

The Complete Works of Oscar Wilde, edited by Vyvyan Holland (London and Glasgow: Collins, 1968) has been used as an easily available and compact edition for all references except those to Wilde's critical works. Here I have used the more complete and easily available *The Artist as Critic: The Critical Writings of Oscar Wilde*, edited by Richard Ellmann (New York: Random House, 1970). All references to Wilde's letters and, of course, *De Profundis* are from *The Letters of Oscar Wilde*, edited by Rupert Hart-Davis (New York: Harcourt, Brace & World, Inc., 1962).

DONALD H. ERICKSEN

Illinois State University

Acknowledgments

Excerpts from *The Letters of Oscar Wilde*, edited by Rupert Hart-Davis, are reprinted by permission of Harcourt Brace Jovanovich Inc.; © 1962 by Vyvyan Holland. Excerpts from *De Profundis* are reprinted by permission of Philosophical Library, Inc. I would like to thank Professor Donald Smalley of the University of Illinois for his initial encouragement in this project. A very special kind of thanks are due David, Susan, Peter, and Jean, who helped me in countless ways. Finally, I would like to express my appreciation to Illinois State University for the summer research grant that enabled me to utilize the superb resources of the William Andrews Clark Library.

Chronology

1895   *An Ideal Husband* and *The Importance of Being Earnest* produced. Wilde tried and sentenced to two years hard labor May 25.

1896   *Salome* produced in Paris. Lady Wilde died.

1897   *De Profundis* written at Reading Gaol. Released from imprisonment May 19. Went to France, never to return to England.

1898   *The Ballad of Reading Gaol* published. Constance Wilde died.

1900   Died in Hotel d'Alsace, Paris.

CHAPTER 1

Life and Times

FEW men in the long history of English literature have had the opportunity, and the misfortune, of assessing their lives and careers from the solitude of a jail cell. Writing to Lord Alfred Douglas in 1897 from Reading Gaol, Oscar Wilde offered these words:

> The gods had given me almost everything. I had genius, a distinguished name, high social position, brilliancy, intellectual daring: I made art a philosophy, and philosophy an art: I altered the minds of men and the colours of things: there was nothing I said or did that did not make people wonder: I took the drama, the most objective form known to art, and made it as personal a mode of expression as the lyric or the sonnet, at the same time that I widened its range and enriched its characterization: drama, novel, poem in rhyme, poem in prose, subtle or fantastic dialogue, whatever I touched I made beautiful in a new mode of beauty: to truth itself I gave what is false no less than what is true as its rightful province, and showed that the false and the true are merely forms of intellectual existence. I treated Art as the supreme reality, and life as a mere mode of fiction: I awoke the imagination of my century so that it created myth and legend around me: I summed up all systems in a phrase, and all existence in an epigram.[1]

These words from Wilde's famous *De Profundis* letter are surely not those of a humble and chastened man but those of a defiant artist intensely conscious of his cultural role as an innovator in art. The reader, after making some allowances for authorial hubris, must grant most of these claims for serious literary attention. Oscar Wilde, the man and the artist, was much more than a brilliant but unaccountable genius whose light was extinguished by a suffocating Philistine society. On the contrary, he was an important artist very much in the mainstream of the intellectual currents of his time, a man clearly aware of what he was trying to achieve in terms of his life and his art.

Oscar Fingal O'Flahertie Wills Wilde[2] was born October 16, 1854, at 21 Westland Row in Dublin. He was the son of William Robert Wills Wilde and Jane Francesca Elgee. His father, Sir William Wilde, as he later became known, was one of the most famous surgeons and oculists of his day. He founded a hospital for the treatment of diseases of the eye and ear and quickly became successful and famous. Such notable figures as the Emperor Maximilian, the King of Sweden, and Queen Victoria utilized his medical services, and in 1864 he was knighted. While still in his twenties, he accompanied a wealthy patient on a trip to the Mediterranean where his contact with pyramids, tombs, mummys, and other artifacts stimulated a lifelong interest in archaeology and archaeological research. Upon his return he wrote a book[3] describing his travels and spoke before several scientific societies. He became popular as a lecturer and at the age of twenty-four was elected a member of the Royal Irish Academy. Unfortunately, his success with patients was almost matched, in a sense, by his success with women although he was not a particularly attractive man. His proclivities toward amorous adventures placed severe strains upon the Wilde household.

Jane Francesca Elgee was the daughter of a solicitor from Wexford who named his daughter Francesca possibly to suggest Italian ancestry. But one certain and certainly distinguished ancestor from Jane's side was Charles Maturin, the author of the Gothic novel *Melmoth the Wanderer* (1820), a book that Wilde drew upon when he wrote *The Picture of Dorian Gray*. Jane Francesca, who spoke French and Italian fluently, was a kind of child prodigy. At the age of twenty she had translated *Sidonia the Sorceress* from the German, but she was best known as a writer of poems and patriotic articles which she published under the pseudonyms "John Fenshaw Ellis" and "Speranza." When an article entitled *Jacta Alea Est* appeared in *The Nation* in July 1848, calling for the people of Ireland to revolt, the paper was suppressed; and Gavan Duffy, a leader of the Young Ireland party, was prosecuted for sedition and high treason. At his trial, when the government read passages from two of Speranza's articles and called for Duffy's conviction on that basis, Jane Francesca Elgee rose angrily and majestically in court to claim authorship of the articles: "I alone am the culprit, I wrote the offending article." The jury could not agree upon a verdict and Jane became a national heroine. Sir William Wilde became enamored of the tall, statuesque national heroine and married her on November 12, 1851.

Their first son, Willie, was born towards the end of 1852 and was soon followed by a second son, Oscar, born on October 16, 1854.[4] Five years after Oscar's birth a daughter, Isola Francesca, was born to Jane and William. When Isola, who was idolized by the family, died in 1867 at the age of eight, the family and, in particular, Oscar were inconsolable. Willie went to Trinity and was later admitted to the Bar. Apparently tiring of the law, he soon abandoned his legal pursuits and became a well-known journalist in London.

Of Oscar's early childhood little seems to be known. His biographers agree that after the birth of Willie, Jane desperately wanted a girl. Thus, when Oscar was born she lavished much of her attention upon him and apparently fulfilled part of this longing by dressing him for a time in girl's clothing.[5] Oscar was a tall, rather awkward boy who disliked the rough games commonly played by other boys. Both Willie and Oscar, as soon as they could manage a knife and fork, were usually present at dinners in the Wilde household. No doubt some of Oscar Wilde's gift for conversation stemmed from his frequent and early contact with the conversation of adults. Jane entertained frequently in their fashionable house at 1 Merion Square. The guests represented a wide assortment of personages gathered from the Irish literary and social world and whatever travelers were passing through Dublin. Discussions and storytelling sometimes lasted until dawn and the Wilde children were seldom excluded. Jane Wilde expected great things of her son for she would say "I am not anxious about Willie, he has a well-shaped head, but I expect simply extraordinary things of Oscar."[6]

At the age of ten Oscar was sent to the Portora Royal School, Enniskillen. His brother Willie had preceded him there and had earned popularity by means of his fists and his gift for conversation, but Oscar was a different sort of boy—large, awkward, and inclined towards dreaming. He became known, however, for his storytelling gifts and his ability to create comic nicknames. Willie was considered the better student by his teachers, but Oscar, who was a voracious reader, managed to win a scholarship at Trinity College, Dublin.

On October 10, 1871, Oscar Wilde entered Trinity and gradually began to reveal his gifts as a student. Although he continued to show little interest or aptitude for such quantitative studies as mathematics, he soon revealed his keen interest in the classics by winning several academic prizes, the most important of which was the Berkeley Gold Medal for Greek, a prize which served him well throughout his life, for he repeatedly pawned it when hard up for funds.[7] No doubt one of the most significant personal influences upon young Oscar Wilde at this time came from the Reverend John Pentland Mahaffy, a professor of ancient history and Wilde's tutor and teacher of Greek. Mahaffy's love of the beauties of Hellenistic culture and landscape was transmitted to Oscar along with his belief in the importance of wit and conversation. Wilde's professor had polished his own gifts until he had become a remarkable talker. Under his tutelage Wilde became an excellent student of the classics and won a demyship worth ninety-five pounds a year at Magdalen College, Oxford.

Oscar Wilde entered Magdalen College on October 17, 1874. The next few years were to be important ones for Oscar for he was to encounter two men who were to have a profound influence on his thought. The first was John Ruskin, Slade Professor of Art, whose *Modern Painters* (1843–1860), *Stones of Venice* (1851–53), and various other works had earned him increasing fame as a writer and lecturer on art. Ruskin warned of the dangers of technology and extolled the nobility of labor. Part of Ruskin's appeal to the young no doubt stemmed from his attempts to put his ideas into practice. The Hinksey experiment in road-making, for example, was a practical application of his belief that labor ought to be noble and useful. In the winter of 1874 Ruskin and a group of Oxford undergraduates tried to build a road across the great swamp that lay between the villages of Lower and Upper Hinksey. Wilde described the experiment during his American tour: "So out we went, day by day, and learned how to lay levels and dig and break stone and to wheel barrows along a plank. Ruskin worked with us in the mist and the rain of an Oxford winter, and our friends and enemies came out and mocked us, but we did not mind them much, and . . . worked away for two months at that road."[8]

Although the project was never finished and resulted in a road that was "about the worst in the country,"[9] the effect upon Wilde was important. From Ruskin's ideas and example sprang a good portion of Wilde's concern for social questions and his awareness of the necessary connection between art and English life. As Wilde himself expressed it," . . . I felt that if there was enough spirit among the young men to go out to such work as road-making for the sake of a noble ideal of life, I could from them create an artistic movement that might change, as it has changed, the face of England."[10] The influence of Ruskin's medievalism, his worship of art and beauty, and his concern for social usefulness were to influence Oscar throughout his artistic life.

But the most important influence at Oxford was Walter Pater, Fellow at Brasenose College and the writer of the sensational *Studies in the History of the Renaissance* (1873). Pater's skepticism and the belief that followed, that the study of one's private experience is more fruitful than the study of a chaotic external world, represented an exciting contrast to conventional social and moral wisdom. For a sensitive young undergraduate like Wilde to learn that the aim of life is to cultivate the deepest response to what is beautiful, profound, or curious is to place before him an irresistibly attractive way of life. Moreover, Pater's ideas seemed to confirm ideas and attitudes already developed. Oscar's eye for what was romantic and picturesque in experience, his distrust of reason, his love for the Romantic poets and such contemporaries as Charles Algernon Swinburne and Walt Whitman, his fascination with the Pre-Raphaelites, his interest in the external beauties of Catholicism rather than its doctrines, all of these, combined with his own skepticism, could be incorporated into Pater's Impressionism.

Wilde loved his years at Oxford and spoke often of them in later life. His letters are filled with the usual anecdotes and observations about clothes, religion, poets, food, parties, lawn tennis (a sport at which Wilde felt he was very good), scholarly prizes, travel, poetry, and people. He also began to live the dandiacal life at Oxford and began his practice of dressing fashionably and flamboyantly. The paneled walls of his rooms were hung with engravings of nudes, a more exceptional practice then than it is today. More significant perhaps was his well-known collection of blue china and his equally famous remark about it: "Oh, would that I could live up to my blue china!" In terms of his artistic credo this was a perfectly sensible statement but it was thought strange at the time.

When young Oscar received his bachelor of arts degree November 28, 1878, he as yet had no clear plans for his life. David Hunter Blair recollects a comment by Wilde at one of the many intimate talks at Oxford that is revealing and prophetic. When asked about his ambitions Wilde replied: "God knows! I won't be a dried-up Oxford don, anyhow. I'll be a poet, a writer, a dramatist. Somehow or other I'll be famous, and if not famous I'll be notorious. Or perhaps . . . I'll rest and do nothing . . . These things are on the knees of the gods. What will be, will be."[11] To fulfill these dreams Wilde went to London as literary hopefuls had done for centuries.

Oscar Wilde's England, that of the second half of the nineteenth century, was enjoying unprecedented economic strength and growth. To most Victorians the soundness of their faith in progress was solidly corroborated by the industrial wonders of the Great Exhibition of 1851. To most Englishmen its exhibits of machinery and the products of machinery further buttressed their faith in England and its material progress. After all, since the repeal of the Corn Laws in 1846 free trade was enriching the nation. Agriculture together with trade and industry were flourishing. The railways were extending themselves over all of England. The colonies, many now existing as self-governing entities bound to the mother country by the "silver thread" of loyalty to the Empire, were creating vast new markets for English manufacturing. At home the various Factory Acts were steadily improving the lot of the working classes by such measures as abolishing child labor and limiting the hours of employment. These measures, combined with other social legislation and the rising of real wages, made the average Victorian confident in his own and the national future.

To Englishmen at the time of Oscar Wilde's birth the nation's economic strength was matched only by its political strength. The Chartist threat in 1848 had led to reform rather than revolution. The national political parties, badly split by the controversy over the passage of the Corn Laws in 1846, had entered upon an era of short ministries that was to last until well beyond the passage of the Second Reform Bill in 1867. The Crimean blunder in 1853 had not really affected England; and the Empire, under the guidance of an enlightened colonial theory and the encouragement of such diverse leaders as Benjamin Disraeli and William Gladstone, in spite of such momentary setbacks as the Indian Mutiny in 1857, continued to develop and prosper. On the whole, England's institutions were working well. The fifties, for most Englishmen, were good times in which to live. Above all of this, as symbols of the national success and the living embodiments of middle-class respectability, stood Queen Victoria and Prince Albert.

The closing decades of the nineteenth century may seem, at first glance, to represent a continuation of the prosperity and satisfaction of the 1850s and 1860s. However, serious economic depressions in 1873 and 1874 shook the confidence of many who had felt that economic prosperity would ascend in a never-ending spiral. A little more than a decade after the passage of the Second Reform Bill in 1867, a third political force, the Labour Party, was added to the traditional Conservative and Liberal alignment. Some of these new leaders shared the socialist-idealist ideas of John Ruskin while others, like William Morris, were attracted to the more revolutionary ideas of Karl Marx and Friedrich Engels. Both Ruskin and Morris felt that the middle classes had become corrupt and no longer capable of responsible leadership. Meanwhile, Bismarck's easy defeat of France in 1871 made many Englishmen uneasily aware that military and industrial competition could threaten England's naval and imperial preeminence.

But the sense of unrest that intensified during the closing decades of the century had deeper roots than economic and political uncertainty. The Victorians, who had inherited a set of religious beliefs based on faith rather than reason, found those beliefs threatened from several directions. The Higher Criticism of the Bible, a scientific-historical approach to Biblical events, aroused great interest and consternation in England. The church was ill equipped or disposed to deal with such threats. Science, especially geology and biology, was also chipping away at the older faith. Even before Charles Darwin's disturbing *Origin of Species* (1859) appeared, its threatening evolutionary thesis had already been set forth in such works as Herbert Spencer's *The Development Hypothesis* (1852). The struggle by Victorian intellectuals to maintain religious belief in the face of such relentless scientific inquiry represents one of the central themes in Victorian literature. For decades perceptive men had long sensed that religious life had become perfunctory and empty, that national ideals had become ever more material, and that everyday life had become monotonous and ugly. First Thomas Carlyle and then Matthew Arnold had attempted to make their countrymen aware of the shortcomings of an era dominated by Philistine culture and values.

The Aesthetic Movement of which Wilde was soon to become the representative figure, was essentially a reaction against the ascendance of what Arnold called "Philistinism" in art and life. Corre-

sponding to the political rise of the masses of Englishmen was an
increasing democratization and vulgarization of styles and tastes that
offended the sensibilities of the more cultivated minority. The reaction against thsee developments was hardly new. Alfred Tennyson
in his "Palace of Art" (1832) expressed the desire to escape the world
of common affairs and dwell alone with art. Matthew Arnold had
struggled with the issue in such poems as "The Strayed Reveller"
(1849) and "Empedocles" (1852). But in the works of each of these
men, the artist renews a commitment, as Jerome Buckley correctly
argues, to the general idea of "morality in art."[12] Nevertheless, art
and life had not, as Ruskin had hoped, fused in England. The attraction of Pater's ideas for sensitive young men like Oscar Wilde are
not difficult to understand, as C. F. Harrold points out, in the light
of these profound changes in economic, political, and religious life:

They saw in Pater's spirit the modern awareness of university relativity, the
rejection of systems of thought, the consciousness that habit is death, the
conviction that only experience—sensations, and memories, and vivid
thoughts—could be real in a world of flux; and that in such a world, where
so much was gross and superfluous, there was an endless opportunity for
delicate choices. Whereas Carlyle had bidden men to work, to bring order
into the world, and to serve a mysterious Divine Idea lying half-legible in
their environment, and within themselves, Pater presented a New
Epicureanism, a withdrawal from the world's brawls. In Pater the Victorian
age shows its fatigue.[13]

This *fin de siècle*[14] weariness found its first expression in the
Aesthetic Movement, although dissatisfactions with Victorian culture had found earlier expression in the Pre-Raphaelites. This grow-
ing severance between art and life, with its potential disregard of
moral concerns, was the source of the virulence of Dickens' satirization of the Pre-Raphaelites and the "art for art's sake" movement in
the character of Harold Skimpole in *Bleak House* (1851).[15] Charles
Dickens was anticipating the young "aesthetes" of the "1880s" like
Oscar Wilde, who rejected any formal ethical aesthetic. The only
obligation of the artist was to cultivate his own individual impressions of the world.

But the Aesthetic Movement was not a "movement" in the same
sense as the Pre-Raphaelites. The aesthetes did not represent a
group with a certain set of aims. Such artists, writers, and thinkers
as John Ruskin, William Morris, Walter Pater, James McNeill

Whistler, Edward Burne-Jones, Algernon Charles Swinburne, and Dante Gabriel Rossetti each represented part of this rebellion against the conventional ideas and tastes of the time, especially the Victorian tendency to insist that art be morally uplifting. Nor was the influence of these aesthetes confined to the eighties. They left their mark, as Jerome Buckley points out, on artists of later decades:

. . . the "aesthetic" regard for craftsmanship remained the controlling force behind many a serious and powerful work of art, from the subtle moral geometrics of James to the enormous intellectual labyrinths of Joyce. And—apart from all formal concerns—there persisted the "aesthetic" concept of the artist as specialist, working with his own symbols in his own difficult medium, defiant of the wide and widening public that was ever less prepared to fathom his particular intention.[16]

When young Oscar Wilde arrived in London he had already been swept up by these intellectual and artistic currents. But his concern at this time was finding the means of achieving personal and literary fame. In the autumn of 1879 he shared rooms at 13 Salisbury Street with Frank Miles, an Oxford friend who was rapidly becoming known for his drawings of beautiful women.[17] The best known of these was Lilly Langtry, whom Miles helped to make famous. Both men shared in the weekly gatherings of celebrities in Wilde's downstairs quarters. Wilde's frequent contacts with the titled and wealthy gave him glimpses into a world of wealth, beauty, luxury, and privilege that were to influence him and his art profoundly. The possibilities of a life shaped, however artificially, from the materials that such a world could provide, no doubt intrigued the young disciple of Pater.

Wilde, partly by accident and partly by design, quickly became the leader among the aesthetic figures of the time. In August of 1880 he moved with Frank Miles to Keats House, Tite Street, Chelsea, for reasons of economy. But that same year his mother arrived in London with Willie and took up quarters in a house in Chelsea. Each Sunday Speranza entertained in her drawing room those persons of literary reputation, however slight, that would accept her invitations. Oscar, of course, was frequently to be seen at his mother's salon. In London he was often seen at evening gatherings in such garb as plum-colored velveteen knickerbockers with perhaps a soft loose shirt with a wide turned-down collar, a large flowing green tie, and black silk stockings. Wilde became notorious for his dress and famous for his outrageous and witty conversation. He was so well known in 1881 that he was the object of satire in Gilbert and Sullivan's *Patience*, an immensely popular opera on "aestheticism." The character Reginald Bunthorne most resembles Wilde, at least he has the best "aesthetic" lines:

> Though the Philistines may jostle, you will rank as an
>   apostle in the high aesthetic band,
> If you walk down Piccadilly with a poppy or a lily
>   in your mediaeval hand.

Wilde, not at all offended by the play, laughed as heartily as anyone. He desired this kind of fame for it provided one means to make money. Hesketh Pearson gives an account of the story that Wilde, attempting to publish his poems before he achieved his notoriety, failed to interest a single publisher. However, immediately upon his lionization his poems were accepted, although he had to bear the expenses of publication, and five editions sold out rapidly.[18] Wilde quickly learned that "nothing succeeds like excess."

Gilbert and Sullivan's opera *Patience*, having enjoyed great success in London, was scheduled to open in New York on September 22, 1882. The producers felt that a lecture tour by Oscar Wilde, the great Aesthete, would give the opera very desirable publicity. Accordingly, Wilde was booked for a series of lectures, the first entitled "The English Renaissance," beginning in New York on January 9, 1882. Wilde arrived in America on the second of January wearing a bottle-green fur-lined overcoat with a fur collar, yellow kid gloves, and a round sealskin cap. When asked whether he had anything to declare, he replied, "I have nothing to declare except my genius." His fame in the United States was instantaneous.

Each city and place that he visited became the occasion for some memorable comment. "Washington," he remarked, "has too many bronze generals." Niagara Falls he described as "simply a vast unnecessary amount of water going the wrong way and then falling over unnecessary rocks." After visiting such major cities in the East as Philadelphia, Boston, Cincinnati, Chicago, and St. Louis, he extended his lecture tour to the West. He spoke in such places as Rockford, Sioux City, Omaha, San Francisco, Salt Lake City, Denver, and Leadville. He returned to the East for more lectures and then visited the South. His tour was a substantial success although his audiences at first seemed to expect to be entertained rather than instructed. In all he delivered more than eighty lectures and did well financially. He made the acquaintance of such noted Americans as Oliver Wendell Holmes, Julia Ward Howe, Harriet Beecher Stowe, Henry Wadsworth Longfellow, Louisa May Alcott, Ulysses S. Grant, Jefferson Davis, Joaquin Miller, Henry Ward Beecher, and Walt Whitman. Oscar's impressions of America are summed up in his comment that "When good Americans die they go to Paris. When bad Americans die they stay in America." On December 27, Wilde sailed for England.

After returning from his American lecture tour, Wilde spent the next three months in Paris where he came to know such artists and writers as Stephen Mallarmé, Paul Verlaine, Alphonse Daudet, Victor Hugo, Edmond de Goncourt, Camille Pissarro, Emile Zola, Henri de Regnier, Edgar Degas, and Gustave Moreau. Wilde audaciously made a number of these acquaintanceships by sending autographed copies of his poetic works. He completed "The Harlot's House" and also worked on "The Sphinx," which he eventually published in 1894. In style and subject matter both poems show the influence of French literary ideas. Wilde, of course, always felt an affinity with France. He liked the tight organization of the world of French letters, the superior brilliance of French theater, the extravagant world of money and fashion, and especially the more open, less inhibited style of living. Soon, however, Oscar ran out of funds and returned to London in May of 1883, where he once again devoted himself to making money. He lectured for a time on "The House Beautiful," "The Value of Art in Modern Life," and, his most popular topic, "Personal Impressions of America."[19]

Wilde's friendship with James McNeill Whistler began about this time. Whistler was twenty years older than Wilde and so much an egotist and so sensitive to criticism that it is unlikely that their friendship could have survived had he read Wilde's comments on his two *Nocturnes* in the review of 1877 of the Grosvenor Gallery Exhibition: "These pictures are certainly worth looking at for about as long as one looks at a real rocket, that is, for somewhat less than a quarter of a minute."[20] Nevertheless, part of the attraction these two men felt for each other derived from their similar attitudes towards the art and artists of the day. Whistler advocated an "art for art's sake" aesthetic that went well beyond even Wilde's views.

Whistler's "Ten O'Clock" lecture delivered in 1885 repudiated not
only the Philistines but the ideals of Ruskin who felt that art and life
should fuse in English life. Whistler also deplored the vulgarization
of the arts by the Aesthetics, whose dilettantism he felt cheapened
what ought to be reserved for the true artist alone. But two men so
devoted to the cultivation of their individuality could not long remain friends. Whistler took offense at any criticism that was unflat-
tering such as Wilde's statement in his review of Whistler's "Ten
O'Clock" lecture: "For that he is indeed one of the greatest masters
of painting is my opinion. And I may add that in this opinion Mr.
Whistler himself entirely concurs."[21]

During the autumn of 1883 Oscar Wilde became engaged to Constance Lloyd, the daughter of an Irish barrister. They had met at a
party in 1881 and had been immediately attracted to each other.
Constance was a shy, sensitive, and very pretty young girl with
beautiful violet eyes who, upon the death of her grandfather with
whom she lived, would inherit an estate of a thousand pounds per
year. She loved Oscar very much and every bit of evidence reveals
that Oscar loved her just as deeply. They were married May 29,
1884. Wilde's many satiric comments about marriage in his plays
had no basis in his marriage. Constance was a loyal wife and, though
shocked at the revelations at his trial, effected a legal separation only
upon the repeated urgings of her friends and relations. One of the
saddest consequences of Wilde's tragedy was that he was separated
from his two sons whom he loved deeply. Constance died April 7,
1898, at Genoa.

When Oscar Wilde married he was thirty years of age and, though
he was widely known and had produced a volume of poems and
several unsuccessful plays, he was without any dependable source of
income. His wife's small income of several hundred pounds a year
was helpful, but not enough to support Oscar's extravagant tastes.
After another lecture tour in England and Scotland, Wilde obtained
a job early in 1885 reviewing books for the *Pall Mall Gazette*. About
the same time he became a drama critic for the *Dramatic Review*.
The birth of his first son, Cyril, June 5, 1885, and his second son,
Vyvyan, November 3, 1886, placed further financial strains on his
household. In 1887 he became editor of *The Lady's World* which
was soon enlarged and renamed *The Woman's World*. Wilde wrote
scores of reviews of contemporary literature and art and persuaded
many of his acquaintances to contribute to his magazine. While
editor of *The Woman's World*, a post he retained until June 1889, he

wrote and published the four short stories that were later collected and published in 1891 under the title *Lord Arthur Savile's Crime and Other Stories*. In 1888 he published *The Happy Prince and Other Tales*, a volume which contained his most successful and enduringly popular stories.

The ambitions that Oscar Wilde had spoken of at Oxford began to be realized. In June of 1890 he sold *The Picture of Dorian Gray* in abbreviated serial form to *Lippincott's Monthly Magazine*. In 1891 his collection of critical essays was published under the title of *Intentions*. This was followed by *A House of Pomegranates*, his third volume of short stories. Moreover, the enlarged *Picture of Dorian Gray* appeared in book form. If we add to this remarkable year the appearance of his provocative essay "The Soul of Man Under Socialism" and the production of his *Duchess of Padua*, we have ample evidence that Oscar Wilde had found his niche in the literary world.

But his period of greatest success began in February of 1892 with the production of *Lady Windermere's Fan*, the first of his society comedies. From this first play he received not only the plaudits of the fashionable public but seven thousand pounds in royalties. Wilde enjoyed another sort of triumph when, in response to the cries for "Author" from the delighted audience, he appeared on stage, cigarette in hand, and said, "Ladies and Gentlemen. I have enjoyed this evening *immensely*. The actors have given us a *charming* rendering of a *delightful* play, and your appreciation has been *most* intelligent. I congratulate you on the *great* success of your performance, which persuades me that you think *almost* as highly of the play as I do."[22] The audience enjoyed this almost as much as Wilde. This triumph was followed by *A Woman of No Importance* in April of 1893. *An Ideal Husband*, yet another success, was produced in January 1895. *The Importance of Being Earnest*, Wilde's most brilliant comedy, was produced in February 1895 and was received with ecstatic delight by both audience and critics.

After Wilde had finished *Lady Windermere's Fan* in the autumn of 1891 he went to France and wrote *Salome*, his great poetic drama. Wilde wrote the drama in French and offered it to Sarah Bernhardt. Rehearsals began in London with the great actress in the lead role. But the Lord Chamberlain refused to license the play on the basis of an old rule stemming from the Reformation that forbade the representation of Biblical characters on the stage. Wilde was furious and protested by declaring his intention of renouncing his British nationality. Wilde, of course, did not carry out his threat; but, although published in book form in England in 1894, the play was never produced in England during Wilde's lifetime.

During these early years of the last decade of the nineteenth century, Oscar Wilde achieved a remarkable degree of success and recognition. Money flooded in from his comedies while his name and the many clever lines from his plays were on everyone's lips. He was lionized by the press and his acquaintance was eagerly sought after by those in aristocratic, social, and artistic circles. He was well known and acclaimed in France and enjoyed a wide circle of friendships there. The extent of Wilde's conquest of the London dramatic world can be grasped when we realize that early in 1895 no fewer than three of his plays, *An Ideal Husband, A Woman of No Importance*, and *The Importance of Being Earnest*, were playing simultaneously in London to rapturous audiences. He had reached the heights like the Faustian and Greek tragic figures that interested him so deeply.

Lionel Johnson, a young poet, introduced Wilde to Lord Alfred Douglas, the third son of the eighth Marquis of Queensberry, in 1891. Douglas was spoiled, high-spirited, willful, and independent. He was twenty-one when he met Wilde and had spent two years at Oxford where he had been an avid lover of sports and literature. Oscar and Lord Alfred quickly became intimate friends. Douglas always denied that there was anything in their relationship beyond certain "familiarities" of friendship,[23] but several of Wilde's letters to Lord Alfred, such as the following one written in January of 1893, led some to think otherwise:

My Own Bosy, Your sonnet is quite lovely, and it is a marvel that those red rose-leaf lips of yours should have been made no less for music of song than for madness of kisses. Your slim gilt soul walks between passion and poetry. I know Hyacinthus, whom Apollo loved so madly, was you in Greek days.

Why are you alone in London, and when do you go to Salisbury? Do go there to cool your hands in the grey twilight of Gothic things, and come here whenever you like. It is a lovely place—it only lacks you; but go to Salisbury first. Always, with undying love, yours . . . (*Letters*, p. 326)

This letter was stolen from Douglas and, among others, later used in an attempt to blackmail Wilde. It was later introduced as evidence in Wilde's trial.[24]

The Marquis of Queensberry was distressed at the increasing notoriety of their friendship and infuriated by (his son's) defiance of his orders to stop seeing Wilde. After a long series of bizarre confrontations, threats, and annoyances, the Marquis left a card at Wilde's Albemarle Club with instructions that the porter deliver it to Oscar. On the card were the words: "To Oscar Wilde posing as a somdomite" (sic).[25] Wilde, who had been repeatedly harassed by the "screaming scarlet Marquis," as Wilde used to call him, finally decided to sue the Marquis for criminal libel. Sir Edward Clarke, a distinguished lawyer, after receiving Wilde's word as an English gentleman that he was innocent of the Marquis' libelous comment, agreed to prosecute the case. The Marquis of Queensberry, meanwhile, busied himself rounding up numbers of male prostitutes and blackmailers as witnesses. The facts suggest that before the case ever went to trial Wilde must have realized that it could go badly with him but, rather than drop the charges or leave the country, he saw the trial through. The trial began the third of April and lasted three days. After the Marquis was acquitted, Wilde's troubles began in earnest. Wilde left the courtroom and drove to the Cadogan Hotel where Lord Alfred had rooms. He was arrested that evening and held without bail until his trial April 26. During the three weeks before his trial he was declared bankrupt and the contents of his house sold at public auction to satisfy Queensberry's petition for court costs. Wilde's first trial ended with a discharged jury, but he was tried again three weeks later. This time he was convicted and sentenced to two years at hard labor.

At the age of forty-one, Oscar Wilde, whose artistic and personal credo was built upon a concern for what is beautiful and rare in human life, found himself denied almost everything that had been meaningful in his life. Except for a one-hour exercise period, he was confined to a whitewashed cell thirteen feet long and seven feet wide for twenty-four hours a day. The only window was six feet nine inches above the floor and prevented even a glimpse of the sky. Wilde's hard labor consisted of picking oakum in his cell.[26] During the first three months of imprisonment he was allowed no books at all except a Bible, a hymnbook, and a prayerbook. Thereafter he was allowed one book a week from the prison library. However, conditions gradually improved.[27] Eventually he was able to obtain books and writing materials to the extent that he could write his famous *De Profundis* letter to Lord Alfred Douglas. When Oscar Wilde's mother became gravely ill, he requested permission to visit her but was refused. Mrs. Wilde died February 3, 1896. Wilde was transferred from Reading Gaol to Pentonville Prison just before his release in order to avoid any confrontation with the Marquis of Queensberry. On his release May 19, 1897, he was met at the gates by Robert Ross,[28] his friend and literary executor.

Oscar Wilde travelled to France that very evening and never again set foot in England. He adopted the name Sebastian Melmoth from the book by his grand-uncle, C. R. Maturin, and after seeing many of his old friends at Dieppe, moved to Berneval and began work on "The Ballad of Reading Gaol" which he finally finished during a trip to Italy with Lord Alfred Douglas. On the seventh of April Constance Wilde died. After a year of wandering about Europe, he returned to Paris in the spring of 1900. He had begun to suffer from increasingly severe headaches. On November 30, 1900, in a room at the Hotel Alsace, Oscar Wilde's life came to an end.

CHAPTER 2

Poetry

" POETRY should be like a crystal, it should make life more beautiful and less real," Oscar Wilde once wrote (*Letters*, p. 217). Of the various pronouncements he made concerning his poetry none is in more perfect harmony with his aesthetic principles. Wilde strove to achieve this crystalline effect in his drama and his fiction as well as in his poetry. But little of the brilliant success in poetic achievement which he so much desired came from the embodiment of this aesthetic idea in his work. Ironically, if we see "The Ballad of Reading Gaol" as the culminating point of Wilde's poetic achievement, as most critics do, then his best and latest work represented an abandonment of his central critical principles.

One can best characterize Wilde's poetry by first separating it into early and late works. The early poetry, represented by "Ravenna" (1878) and *Poems* (1881), is intensely lyrical and heavily imitative of the poetic styles of John Keats, Alfred Tennyson, Dante Gabriel Rossetti, and Algernon Charles Swinburne. In fact, Wilde shows little if any interest in experimentation with new poetic techniques. Much archaic, rather trite poetic diction is blended with catalogues of classical allusions. Sensuous, highly palpable physical qualities predominate in his imagery. There is little symbolism or aesthetic distance in this early poetry, but there is a conscious effort to imitate the Pre-Raphaelite emphasis upon heavy adjectival embroidery or what Edouard Roditi calls "museum-piece ornateness."[1] If we add to these qualities the stressing of descriptive detail, the emphasis upon literary subjects, the effort to create an effect of strangeness, and the detachment from any ethical or utilitarian concerns, Wilde's debt to the Pre-Raphaelites is clear. He differs from them in that the particularity of detail in his poetry is rarely, if ever, emblematic of a spiritual state. Several of the early poems are Impressionistic[2] in that they possess brilliant color combinations, synaesthesia,[3] exact

29

imagery, and the Whistlerian emphasis upon nuances of mood and feeling at the expense of social concerns. Striking examples of Impressionistic poetry are found in such later works as "Impressions: Le Jardin des Tuileries," "Symphony in Yellow," and "Fantaisies Decoratives." More significantly, however, in "The Harlot's House" and "The Sphinx," Wilde discards his derivative Romantic and Pre-Raphaelite style in favor of a poetry that is both Impressionistic and symbolic.

An overall reading of Wilde's poetry also reveals a shift in thematic concerns from the general discussions of political liberty, social injustice, and aesthetic and moral issues found in the early works to the personal aesthetic impressions and moral conflicts in the later poetry. But Oscar Wilde, as Jerome Buckley points out, seemed to lack faith in his own creations.[4] Except for a few distinguished works real achievement escaped him. Only in 1898 in his last work, "The Ballad of Reading Gaol," did he achieve the originality, directness, and plain economy that enabled him to write a kind of new poetry that anticipated that of the twentieth century.

I "Ravenna"

Several months after Wilde had won the Newdigate Prize for poetry, he wrote to the Reverend Matthew Russell, S. J., about the "strange coincidence" of his winning the prize: "On the 31st of March 1877 (long before the subject was given out) I entered Ravenna on my way to Greece, and on 31st March 1878 I had to hand my poem in. It is quite the blue ribbon of the Varsity . . ." (Letters, p. 54). Sir Roger Newdigate, who founded the prize in 1806, had stipulated that the poem not exceed fifty lines and that it concern some classical subject. In 1826 these regulations were modified. The poem could now be any length and "of late years laxity is allowed from the horrid Popeian jingle of regular heroics . . ." (Letters, p. 53).

Wilde's "Ravenna" consists of 332 lines of decasyllabic couplets divided into seven sections that describe his various responses to his first glimpse of this ancient Italian city: "O how my heart with boyish passions, burned,/When far away across the sedge and mere/ I saw the Holy City rising clear . . ."[45] The history of Ravenna has been filled with greatness, for here are buried "huge-limbed Theodoric, the Gothic king"; Gaston de Foix, "The Prince of Chivalry, the Lord of War"; Dante, with "The lips that sang of

Heaven and of Hell"; and finally, Lord Byron "a second Anthony/
Who of the world another Actium made!" But the poet finds that
this city in which the "Great of Time" are buried, is now "strangely
still" (ll. 37, 59–150). Although her sisters in glory—Rome, Naples,
Venice, Genoa, and Milan—are thriving, Ravenna lies asleep:

> Weary of life, thou liest in silent sleep,
> As one who marks the lengthening shadows creep,
> Careless of all the hurrying hours that run,
> Mourning some day of glory, for the sun
> Of Freedom hath not shewn to thee his face,
> And thou hast caught no flambeau in the race. (ll. 233-238)

At the poem's close, the poet expresses his sorrow in Keatsian terms
at taking leave, albeit imaginative, of the city of his inspiration:

> Adieu, Ravenna! but a year ago,
> I stood and watched the crimson sunset glow
> From the lone chapel on thy marshy plain:
> The sky was as a shield that caught the stain
> Of Blood and battle from the dying sun . . .
> . . . .
> Adieu! Adieu! yon silver lamp, the moon,
> Which turns our midnight into perfect noon,
> Doth surely light thy towers, guarding well
> Where Dante sleeps, where Byron loved to dwell.
> (ll. 293–297, 329–332)

The poem with which Wilde won the Newdigate Prize, a prize
which Arnold and Ruskin had won before him, is the work of a
talented but as yet highly derivative poet. Wilde's repeated use of
the word "weary" in section six or the references to "that fatal
weed/Which makes a man forget his fatherland" in section two, too
obviously suggest Tennyson's "Mariana" and "The Lotus Eaters."
The unmistakable voice of Keats is heard in the tone of "Adieus" of
the closing section of the poem. Wilde's adaptations of Homeric
epithets into English forms reveals the influence, probably indirect,
of Anglo-Saxon poetry and William Morris's translations of Homer.[6]
Thus, Theodoric is "huge-limbed," the galleys are "pine-forest-
like," the ships are "brass-beaked."

Wilde even borrowed from his own poems. Whole lines from his
earlier "Magdalen Walks," and "The Grave of Keats" are incorpo-

rated into "Ravenna." But the poem is more than what Boris Brasol calls a "pseudo-classical rhetoric composition"[7] or Epifanio San Juan a "mechanized travelogue."[8] It is, as Arthur Ransome maintains, "an admirable prize poem."[9] Its poetic merits are limited, but it represents a substantial poetic achievement for a twenty-two-year-old Oxford undergraduate.

II Poems

Wilde's career as a poet really begins with his *Poems*, published in 1881 just three years after he won the Newdigate prize at Oxford. After Wilde's arrival in London, he endeavored to follow up this early poetic triumph at Oxford with the publication of a full-scale volume of poetry. Hesketh Pearson recounts the story that Wilde had attempted to publish his *Poems* well before 1881 but had been turned down repeatedly. Only when he had become a social lion could he get his works published.[10] The lesson that success as a celebrity, dandy, and Aesthete was necessary in order to provide a market for his artistic goods was apparently not lost on Oscar.

Five editions of his poetry sold out rapidly, but the reaction of the critical "establishment" could hardly have been less encouraging to the young poet. Oliver Elton's arguments to the Oxford Union Debating Society for returning the presentation copy that Wilde had sent suggest the tone of many of the early reviews:

> It is not that these poems are thin—and they *are* thin, it is not that they are immoral—and they *are* immoral: it is not that they are this or that—and they *are* all this and all that: it is that they are for the most part not by their putative father at all, but by a number of better-known and more deservedly reputed authors. They are in fact by William Shakespeare, by Philip Sidney, by John Donne, by Lord Byron, by William Morris, by Algernon Swinburne, and by sixty more, whose works have furnished the list of passages which I hold in my hand at this moment. The Union Library contains better and fuller editions of all these poets: the volume which we are offered is theirs, not Mr. Wilde's: and I move that it be not accepted.[11]

The book was not accepted by the Society. If Elton's judgment was harsh, the judgments of the influential *Spectator, Athenaeum,* and *Saturday Review* were even harsher. The *Spectator* maintained that "If Mr. Wilde were a less clever man, we should think less badly of his book. But, it is clear he must and does know how artificial and pumped-up it is. . . ."[12] The *Athenaeum* was most unfavorably impressed by "the over-indulgence of metaphor, in affected neologisms, and in conceits behind which sense and reason are obscured."[13] The *Saturday Review* maintained that "The book is not without traces of cleverness, but is marred everywhere by imitation, insincerity and bad taste."[14]

Wilde's volume of verse is arranged in a sonata or symphony pattern.[15] There are four "movements" or clusters of short poems that are separated by much longer poems. The first two sections are entitled "Eleutheria" and "Rosa Mystica." The third consists of three groupings entitled "Wind Flowers," "Flowers of Gold," and "Impressions du Théatre." The last grouping is called "The Fourth Movement." This phrase was added to the table of contents in the revised edition of 1882. The analogy to a symphonic composition is reinforced by the positioning of "Helas!" at the opening of his volume. This sonnet with its concern for the destruction inflicted upon the poet's soul by his willingness to "drift with every passion" establishes the "keynote" of Wilde's volume.

Wilde once described his "keynote" sonnet as his most characteristic poem.[16] Unlike the other poems in the volume, "Helas!" is printed in italics to emphasize its importance in terms of the overall subject of the volume—the revelation of the personality of the poet. The sonnet's opening lines strike a note that was to become familiar not only in this volume but in his later work as well:

> *To drift with every passion till my soul*
> *Is a stringed lute on which all winds can play,*
> *It is for this that I have given away*
> *Mine ancient wisdom and austere control?* (ll. 1-4)

Throughout his career Wilde thought of himself in these romantic terms. The closing note of withdrawal and loss is capped by the speaker's regret that he must "lose a soul's inheritance." "Helas!" to anyone familiar with Wilde's life has a curious prophetic quality. Wilde seems aware even at this early date of the later tragedy that awaited him.

The first grouping of poems in the 1881 edition is entitled "Eleutheria" ("freedom, liberty"). Of the eight poems, six are sonnets. But these initial poems reveal little of the concern for artistic methods, attitudes, or subject matter that we might expect of the leading "aesthetic" personality of the age. Wilde's "Sonnet to Lib-

erty," probably the best of the group, expresses the extent of the
poet's sympathies with the turmoils that accompany political struggles for liberty:

> . . . the roar of thy Democracies,
> Thy reigns of terror, thy great Anarchies,
> Mirror my wildest passions like the sea
> And give my rage a brother . . . (ll. 4-7).

Wilde denied that this sonnet expressed his political creed,[17] but
the closing lines with their reference to Christ suggest a closer
kinship perhaps than Wilde was willing to admit. The other poems
are also concerned with political subjects. "Ave Imperatrix," enthusiastically praised by American reviewers, reveals in its thirty-
one four-line stanzas the poet's concern that "England with bare and
bloody feet/Climbs the steep road of wide empire" (ll. 35-36) and
sends many of her brothers into early and distant graves. Although
the poet laments that "Wild grasses are their burial-sheet/And sobbing waves their threnody" (ll. 111-112), he apparently accepts the
idea of empire for "Up the steep road must England go" (l. 120).
Wilde's sonnet "To Milton" is notable only because of its heavy
borrowing from Wordsworth's "London, 1802." "Louis Napoleon,"
the other non-sonnet, is undistinguished as are his "Sonnet on the
Massacre of the Christians in Bulgaria," "Quantum Mutata," and
"Libertatis Sacra Fames." In the last sonnet, "Theoretikos," the
poet touches upon questions relating to art and the artist. On this
occasion, the artist, who now sees that the empire "hath but feet of
clay," exhorts his soul to "escape" this "vile traffic-house" where
"Wisdom and reverence are sold at mart," for in "dreams of Art/And
loftiest culture I would stand apart,/Neither for God, nor for his
enemies" (ll. 1-14). This early disdain for Philistine culture and his
view that art and the artist should stand apart from reality became
dominant artistic stances throughout Wilde's career.
  The first of the long poems that separate the major sections is
entitled "The Garden of Eros." Its forty-six Venus and Adonis stanzas create the artificial pastoral setting that so attracted Wilde in his
early poetry. His emphasis upon excessive adjectival embroidery,
the effort at pictorial effects through particularization, the archaisms, the somewhat trite diction, the frequent classical allusions,

and, most of all, the heavy Keatsian sensuosity make the "Garden of Eros" a representative early poem. In fact, Wilde wrote that next to "The Burden of Itys" he liked "The Garden of Eros" best (*Letters*, p. 217). Following the seventeen opening descriptive stanzas, the poet reassures the Spirit of Beauty that the votaries of such beauty, though few, are not dead in "this starved age" with its "new-found creeds so sceptical and so dogmatical" (ll. 113-114). Wilde's speaker then lists the nineteenth century votaries of the Spirit of Beauty whom he admires: Keats, "the boy who loved thee best"; Shelley; Byron, "whose clear eye/Saw from our tottering throne and waste of war/The grand Greek limbs of young Democracy/Rise mightily"; Swinburne; Morris, "our sweet and simple Chaucer's child"; Rossetti; and Burne-Jones, "Who saw old Merlin lured in Vivien's snare" (ll. 123-218).

The next five stanzas reveal that in spite of such lofty votaries all is not well in Arcady:

> . . . the cheating merchants of the mart
> With iron roads profane our lovely isle,
>   and break on whirling wheels the limbs of Art,
> Ay! through the crowded factories beget
> The blind-worm Ignorance that slays the soul . . . . (ll. 196-200)

Although men can now "prophesy about the sun,/And lecture on his arrows—how, alone,/Through a waste void the soulless atoms run," those who worship the Spirit of Beauty are few "and all romance has flown" (ll. 219-222).

The difference in response revealed by this late nineteenth century poem and Tennyson's "In Memoriam" (1850) to the problem of coming to terms with the nature of science reveals vividly the extent to which Victorian "earnestness" had eroded. Where Tennyson's speaker in "In Memoriam" is dismayed by "nature red in tooth and claw" and "stars that blindly run," Wilde's spokesman sees a world of "Natural Warfare" and "Insensate Chance" (1. 244). Tennyson's speaker, however, concludes with the affirmation that all Nature points toward "one far-off divine event,/To which the whole creation moves." Wilde's spokesman sets aside his social concerns and turns to beauty: "Ah! there is something more in that bird's flight/Than could be tested in a crucible!—" (ll. 275-276). Wilde's "Garden of Eros" reveals the change in just thirty-one years from typical Victorian earnestness to the later nineteenth century tendency towards withdrawal rather than firm commitment to life.

"Rosa Mystica" was the title of the second section containing fourteen poems, most of which concern topics derived from Wilde's travels in Italy. "By the Arno" and "Italia" celebrate the beauties and history of Italy, while others such as "San Maniatao," "Ave Maria Gratia Plene," "Sonnet Written in Holy Week at Genoa," "Rome Unvisited," "Urbs Sacra Aeterna," and "Easter Day" reveal Wilde's fascination with various facets of the Roman church, especially the Virgin. But blended with the religious images in these poems are very sensuous, palpable images of life. The sonnet "Madonna Mia" is interesting mainly because it reveals the influence of the Pre-Raphaelites upon the young poet. Like Rossetti's "Blessed Damozel," her spiritual qualities are strangely mingled with sensuous detail:

> A lily-girl, not made for this world's pain,
>   With brown, soft hair close braided by her ears,
>   And longing eyes half veiled by slumberous tears.
> Like bluest water seen through mists of rain:
> Pale cheeks whereon no love hath left its stain,
> Red underlip drawn in for fear of love,
> And white throat, whiter than the silvered dove,
> Through whose wan marble creeps one purple vein. (ll. 1-8)

Though the poet insists "Even to kiss her feet I am not bold" (l. 10), like the Madonna of Browning's bishop she moves man's earthly self. The poet's intense awareness of the young Madonna's beauty in the octave carries the poet in the sestet to the plane of the spiritual: "Like Dante, when he stood with Beatrice/Beneath the flaming lion's breast, and saw/The seventh Crystal, and the Stair of Gold" (ll. 12–14). Wilde's effort to achieve pictorial effects with heavy adjectival embellishment combined with the strange effect created by his reaching for the spiritual at the same time that he renders the sensuous, suggests the Pre-Raphaelite influence.

The poem that William Butler Yeats chose for *A Book of Irish Verse* (1895) was "Requiescat" (*Letters*, p. 365). Written in memory of Wilde's little sister Isola, who died in 1867 at the age of eight, the poem owes something perhaps to Thomas Hood's "Bridge of Sighs" and Matthew Arnold's "Requiescat." The beauty of Wilde's "Requiescat," the most praised of the pieces in the 1881 volume, stems from the spare, direct language:

> Tread lightly, she is near
> Under the snow,
> Speak Gently, she can hear
> The daisies grow. (ll. 1-4)

The restraint of the final lines, "All my life's buried here,/Heap earth upon it" (ll. 19-20), represents the key to the poem's excellence. Such restraint was unusual for Wilde as he himself was aware.[18] Only in the "Ballad of Reading Gaol" (1898) did he return to such simplicity and directness.

"The Burden of Itys" was, if Wilde's letter to Violet Hunt is to be believed (*Letters*, p. 79), his favorite poem. Wilde uses fifty-eight of the six-line stanzas that he employed in "The Garden of Eros" to express in conventionally pastoral terms the poet's melancholy loss at having no pagan world of deities in which to believe nor anything in modern life to compensate for the loss. Nevertheless, the poet observes that "This English Thames is holier far than Rome" and in ". . . the foam/of meadow-sweet and white anemone" God is "likelier there/Than hidden in that crystal-hearted star the pale/monks hear" (ll. 1-6). Thus he exhorts the lovely bird he hears singing in the English countryside to continue to celebrate beauty:

> Sing on! Sing on! I would be drunk with life,
>   Drunk with the trampled vintage of my youth,
> I would forget the wearying wasted strife,
>   The riven veil, the Gorgon eyes of Truth,
> The prayerless vigil and the cry for prayer,
> The barren gifts, the lifted arms, the dull insensate air! (ll. 235-240)

But the poet realizes at the close of the poem that "It was a dream, the glade is tenantless,/No soft Ionian laughter moves the air,/The Thames creeps on in sluggish leadenness" (ll. 295-297). Evening comes and the landscape fades. At this point, near the end of the poem, the note of estrangement found in "Helas!" and other poems is repeated:

> 'Tis I, 'tis I, whose soul is as the reed
>   Which has no message of its own to play.

So pipes another's bidding, it is I,
Drifting with every wind on the wide sea of misery. (ll. 333-336)

"The Burden of Itys," in spite of its blend of Arnoldian classicism and Keatsian sensuosity, does succeed as a poem. Nevertheless, in this early poetry, Wilde seems unable to find an authentic poetic voice in which to express his ideas.

The third section of Wilde's 1881 volume consists of three related groups of poems titled "Wind Flowers," "Flowers of Gold," and "Impressions du Théatre." Divisions one and two, comprised of seven and thirteen poems respectively, are of particular interest because they reveal Wilde's attempt to write in the Imagist style that he later employed with great success in "The Harlot's House." Wilde's lines, especially those from "Impression Du Matin," are often suggestive of Whistler's titles:

> The Thames nocturne of blue and gold
>   Changed to a Harmony in grey
>   A barge with ochre-coloured hay
> Dropt from the wharf: and chill and cold
> The yellow fog came creeping down
>   The bridges till the houses' walls
>   Seemed changed to shadows and St. Paul's
> Loomed like a bubble o'er the town. (ll. 1-8)

Wilde's effort to create a poetic impression that is analogous to musical forms is related to the efforts of the Pre-Raphaelites to express spiritual states of mind through pictorial details. Wilde differs from the Pre-Raphaelites in that he is less concerned with rendering spiritual states of mind than psychological ones. When the poet says that "Houses' walls/Seemed changed to shadows and St. Paul's/Loomed like a bubble o'er the town," he is describing the altered perceptions and psychological state of his observer. Largely absent is the ornateness of much of his early work while the simplicity and directness of the best of his later poetic work is happily present. Other poems such as "Magdalen Walks," "Athanasia," "Serenade for Music," and "Endymion" reveal the persistence of Wilde's highly sensuous Keatsian style with its forced archaisms. Only "Chanson," a short ballad, possesses the simplicity and restraint which Wilde needed to perfect. In "La Belle Donna Della Mia Mente," in what seems an imitation of Keats' "La Belle Dame

Sans Merci," Wilde created a symbolic figure of intense sensuality described in imagery that suggests his later version of the Biblical Salome: "As a pomegranate, cut in twain,/White-seeded, is her crimson mouth" (ll. 25-26).

"Wind Flowers" and "Flowers of Gold" are separated by the longest poem in Wilde's volume. "Charmides" consists of one hundred and eleven of his variation of the Venus and Adonis stanza. The story goes that when asked if "Charmides" was his favorite poem Wilde is said to have replied "Yes, that is my favourite poem. I think it my best. It is the most perfect and finished."[19] The poem tells the story of Charmides, a Grecian lad who hides himself away in the temple of Athena and lavishes his passion on a statue of the goddess. Later, after the outraged goddess has drowned Charmides in revenge, his body is washed ashore by "some good Triton-God." Thinking him only asleep, a young girl falls in love with his beauty and lavishes her passion upon his body as he had done upon the statue. She is killed by one of Diana's arrows but the Queen of Cythere carries her and Charmides away. Though part of the Underworld now, they are allowed to fulfill their passion:

> Enough, enough that he whose life had been
> A fiery pulse of sin, a splendid shame,
> Could in the loveless land of Hades glean
> One scorching harvest from those fields of flame
> Where passion walks with naked unshod feet
> And is not wounded,—ah! enough that once
> their lips could meet (ll. 655-660).

The style of Wilde's "Charmides" is reminiscent of Keats, Arnold, and Swinburne; but the effect is blurred by the excessively decorative style. The *Saturday Review* was distressed by the explicitness of the passages which described how Charmides "Undid the cuirass, and the crocus gown,/And bared the breasts of polished ivory" (ll. 103-104). The reviewer felt that "So much talk about 'grand cool flanks' and 'crescent thighs' is decidedly offensive."[20]

The twelve poems that comprise the "Flowers of Gold" section vary in purpose and technique. "Theocritus: A Villanelle," "A Vision," and "Amor Intellectualis" are undistinguished poems composed in Wilde's overwrought Keatsian manner. "Les Silhouettes," "La Fuite de la Lune," "In the Gold Room: A Harmony," and "Impression du Voyage" reveal Wilde once again using landscape as

a correspondence for psychological mood. In the case of "In the
Gold Room" he creates images strikingly similar to those of the *Art
Nouveau* movement:

> Her gold hair fell on the wall of gold
> Like the delicate gossamer tangles spun
> On the burnished disk of the marigold,
> Or the sunflower turning to meet the sun
> When the gloom of the jealous night is done,
> And the spear of the lily is aureoled. (ll. 7-12)

Of the remaining poems, "Ballade de Marguerite," "The Dole of the
King's Daughter," "The Grave of Shelley," and "The Grave of
Keats," only the first two are of interest because of Wilde's skillful
employment of ballad conventions. The grouping entitled "Impressions de Théatre" consists of tributes to well-known theatrical personalities of the day.

The third section ends with "Panthea," a long poem consisting of
thirty of the six-line stanzas Wilde used for "The Garden of Eros,"
"The Burden of Itys," "Charmides," and "Humanitad." Wilde's
debt to Walter Pater's *Renaissance* is revealed early in the poem.
The speaker argues that it is better to live pleasurably:

> For, sweet, to feel is better than to know,
> And Wisdom is a childless heritage,
> One pulse of passion—youth's first fiery glow,—
> Are worth the hoarded proverbs of the safe: (ll. 7-10)

This Paterian note is maintained until the thirteenth stanza. Here
Wilde's speaker maintains that we are born too late to "oppress our
natures" and "Starve and feed in vain repentance"; rather, we
"crowd into one finite pulse of time/The joy of infinite love and the
fierce pain of infinite crime" (ll. 73-78). In the next stanza, however,
the Paterian note is replaced by one suggestive of Edward
Fitzgerald's "Rubaiyat." Wilde's speaker argues that, man's guilt
and despair are wearisome and pointless "For man is weak; God
sleeps; and heaven is high; /One Fiery-coloured moment: one great
love; and lo! we die" (ll. 79-84).

The stanzas that follow contain a Wildean species of post-
Darwinian idealism that places his poem in the mainstream of Victo-

rian concern with the religious and scientific implications of evolutionary theory. Wilde closes his sixteenth stanza with the observation that "all life is one, and all is change" and in the stanza that follows attempts, as Tennyson did in his "In Memoriam" (1850), to come to terms with evolutionary thought:

> . . . we are part
> Of every rock and bird and beast and hill,
> One with the things that prey on us, and one with what we kill.
>
> From lower cells of waking life we pass
>   To full perfection; thus the world grows old:
> We who are godlike now were once a mass
>   Of quivering purple flecked with bars of gold,
> Unsentient or of joy or misery,
> And tossed in terrible tangles of some wild
>   and wind-swept sea. (ll. 100-108)

Wilde's speaker continues with a description of the consolation of being forever a part of nature, for after death "Without life's conscious, torturing pain/In some sweet flower we will feel the sun;/And from the linnet's throat will sing again" (ll. 133-135). Thus, at the close of the poem, the reader learns that "the stealthy creeping years/Have lost their terrors now, we shall not die/The Universe itself shall be our Immortality" (ll. 178-180).

If Ransome's dismissal of the poem as "boy's thought"[21] from Swinburne is valid, then Swinburne's "Hertha" (1871) and George Meredith's "Woods of Westermain" (1883) are boy's thought also, for these poems are similar post-Darwinian efforts at coming to terms with the old Victorian problem. The weakness of "Panthea" lies not in the quality of its thought but in Wilde's decoration of his ideas in pretentious pastoral epithets such as "The golden-vestured sun" (l. 43), "wind-stirred lilies" (l. 51), and "diapered fritillaries" (l. 155). Too often his works suffered in varying degrees from this sort of derivative excess.

The fourth division of Wilde's 1881 volume, appropriately entitled "The Fourth Movement," consists of eight poems. The first "Impression: Le Réveillon" was published earlier in 1877 as "Lotus Leaves." The latter part of the title is a painter's term for the employment of strong light against a dark background, an effect Wilde attempted to reproduce in his poem:

> An jagged brazen arrows fall
> Athwart the feathers of the night,
> And a long wave of yellow light
> Breaks silently on tower and hall, . . . (ll. 5-8)

"At Verona" expresses Wilde's admiration for Italy and his sense of exile. "Apologia" contains both this consciousness of exile and a sense of self-transcendence. Of the remaining poems, "Quia Multum Amavi," "Silentium Amoris," "Her Voice," "My Voice," and "Taedium Vitae," only the last is of much interest. In this poem, the last sonnet in the volume, Wilde seems to deplore the necessity, most likely his own, "to wear/This paltry age's gaudy livery,/To mesh my soul within a woman's hair,/And be mere Fortune's lack-eyed groom. . . ." (ll. 1-5).

"Humanitad," the last of the long poems that separate the "movements" of Wilde's volume, represents in seventy-three six-line stanzas a good example of Wilde's early philosophical poetry. The poem begins rather conventionally with a description of a winter landscape which soon changes to one of spring. The poet then invokes the spring which will revise everything in nature except the poet's faith in himself and his age. The poem concludes with Wilde's observation that although mankind throughout its long evolutionary history has been the source of its own crucifixion, it will come down from the cross and reign as God. "Humanitad" is a long and somewhat confused poem in which Wilde expressed several of his continuing social concerns. But Wilde's fascination with Christ as a symbol of suffering and exile is more significant.[22] In the later poetry, with the exception of "The Ballad of Reading Gaol," Wilde muted the social concerns but his interest in Christ intensified.

The last poem in the volume, "Flower of Love," represents another of Wilde's poems based upon the themes of sin, suffering, and remorse. Its fifteen couplets strike an initial note of regret for the poet's failure to achieve poetic greatness.

III "The Harlot's House"

Wilde asserted in his *Pall Mall* review of Whistler's "Ten O'Clock" that ". . . the poet is the supreme artist, for he is the master of colour and form, and the real musician besides, and is lord over all life and all arts; and so to the poet beyond all others are these mysteries known. . . ."[23] "The Harlot's House," according to J. D. Thomas, probably served to illustrate the poetic and artistic ideas Wilde expressed in his review.[24] The poem first appeared in the *Dramatic Review*, April 11, 1885, midway during the five weeks when Whistler was giving his lectures.

"The Harlot's House" is, as Roditi maintains, "The most perfect example of Wilde's mature art as a poet."[25] It consists of twelve three-line stanzas with linked rhymes. The first two lines of each tercet are rhymed while the last line of each tercet rhymes with the last line of the following stanza. The effect is to set the third line apart from the first two and accentuate its function as a commentary. This effect is heightened by a flattening of the rhythm of the third line, as in the seventh tercet:

> Sometimes a clockwork puppet pressed
> A phantom lover to her breast,
> Sometimes they seemed to try to sing. (ll. 19-21)

The poem is structured so as to reach its climax in the last line. This sense of dramatic finality is intensified by shortening this last line by two syllables:

> Then suddenly the tune went false,
> The dancers wearied of the Waltz,
> The shadows ceased to wheel and whirl,
>
> And down the long and silent street,
> The dawn, with silver-sandalled feet,
> Crept like a frightened girl. (ll. 31-36)

In "The Harlot's House" Wilde is writing in the decadent and *fin de siècle* style, with its heavy emphasis upon strange moods and sensory details that were hinted at in several of the poems in the 1881 volume. But the poem also reveals a strong symbolic charge. Although the poem ostensibly deals with the desertion of the poet by his love, its symbolic meaning is of greater significance. It is useful to remember that the poem was apparently published in response to Wilde's controversy with Whistler,[26] for its images make the most sense in terms of Wilde's artistic dicta. What the poet and his love see and hear indistinctly are mainly the discordant sounds of music, the "din and fray" (1.4) of people, and the shadows of "wire pulled automatons" (l. 13) dancing. When they see "a horrible marionette" smoking a cigarette "like a live thing" (ll. 22–24), the poet observes that "The dead are dancing with the dead,/The dust is whirling with the dust" (ll. 26-27). But the poet's love reacts quite differently:

> But she—she heard the violin,
> And left my side, and entered in:
> Love passed into the house of lust. (ll. 28-30)

She succumbs to the same artistic mistake Dorian Gray made when he became enmeshed in the mundane realities of self-gratification and crime. The poet's love becomes entranced by the false images and harmonies of reality or false art, thereby dispelling true beauty as symbolized by the dawn "with silver-sandalled feet" which "Crept like a frightened girl" (ll. 35-36). Thus, as Wilde argues in "The Critic as Artist," the true artist ". . . will prefer to look into the silver mirror, or through the woven veil, and will turn his eyes away from the chaos and clamour of actual existence, though the mirror be tarnished and the veil be torn" ("Critic as Artist," pp. 365-366).

IV "The Sphinx"

According to Stuart Mason, Oscar Wilde is reported to have said that he "hesitated to publish The Sphinx as it would destroy domesticity in England."[27] Although the poem failed of this effect, it does represent one of the earliest of those few instances when Wilde alludes in his poetry to his secret sexual life. The poem was begun at Oxford, completed at Paris in 1883, and steadily revised until its publication in 1894. Charles Ricketts designed the book cover and its striking interior design. Ricketts was apparently pleased with his design, for he referred to it as "the first book of the modern revival printed in three colours."[28]

"The Sphinx" is modelled somewhat after Poe's "The Raven." Like Poe's "Raven" the poem opens in the speaker's quarters with a confrontation, in this case, with a mysterious Sphinx:

> In a dim corner of my room for longer than my
>   fancy thinks
> A beautiful and silent Sphinx has watched me
>   through the shifting gloom.

> Inviolate and immobile she does not rise she does
>   not stir
> For silver moons are naught to her and naught to
>   her the suns that reel. (ll. 1-4)

The rest of the poem's eighty-seven stanzas are concerned mainly with the Sphinx's "thousand weary centuries" of history as they are recalled by the twenty-year-old speaker. The Sphinx becomes the embodiment in the speaker's Byzantine recollection of all the exotic, secret, and forbidden wonders of its past, especially its imagined sexual past:

> Who were your lovers? Who were they who wrestled
>   for you in the dust?
> Which was the vessel of your lust? What Leman
>   had you every day?
>
> Did giant lizards come and crouch before you on
>   the reedy banks?
> Did Gryphons with great metal flanks leap on you
>   in your trampled couch?
>
> Or had you shameful secret guests and did you
>   harry to your home
> Some Nereid coiled in amber foam with curious
>   rock crystal breasts? (ll. 45-54)

After his expression of abhorrence at the Sphinx and the sensuality she represents, the speaker finally takes refuge in the crucifix:

> Get hence, you loathesome mystery! Hideous
>   animal, get hence!
> You wake in me each bestial sense, you make me
>   what I would not be.
>
> You make my creed a barren sham, you wake foul
>   dreams of sensual life,
> And Atys with his blood-stained knife were better
>   than the thing I am.
>
> False Sphinx! False Sphinx! By reedy Styx old
>   Charon, leaning on his oar,
> Waits for my coin. Go thou before, and leave
>   me to my crucifix, . . . (ll. 167-172)

It is perhaps ironic that a poem in which Wilde speaks of "shameful secret guests" should be written in Tennyson's "In Memoriam" form. Wilde converts the quatrains into long couplets with barely concealed internal rhymes. This modification slows the verse and provides an opportunity for internal rhyme and caesura effects that suited Wilde's deliberately florid, Byzantine style. Although the overdone Keatsian imagery of Wilde's earlier poetry is mostly absent, he attempts, with only partial success, some incredible rhymes: "talc" with "Oreichalch," "sarcophagus" with "Tragelophos," or "catafalque" with "Amenalk" (*Letters*, p. 144). Wilde is trying, of course, by employing such rhymes and terms, to create an effect of Oriental strangeness.

With "The Sphinx," just as he does to a lesser extent in "The Harlot's House," "The New Remorse," and other poems, Wilde demonstrated his ability, as Roditi points out, to create the *Fleurs du Mal* of English literature,[29] if he had been willing to take the inevitable risks. Wilde is writing in a similar symbolic mode. The Sphinx, as the opening lines suggest, has been incarnated "inviolate and immobile" (l. 3). She is outside of time or the flux of existence for "silver moons are naught to her" nor "the suns that reel" (l. 4). San Juan maintains that the Sphinx is "a godlike spirit of history,"[30] but the figure is more richly suggestive than that. She is Wilde's symbol for the evil in the world that, through its beauty as well as its ugliness, its fascination as well as its repulsion, has had at times in man's history a seemingly supernatural power. For this reason Wilde balances its power against that of Christianity, thus expressing the eternal struggle between these forces. That the poem had special importance to Wilde is obvious from his letters. Wilde worked with this symbolic idea in other works, most significantly in *Salome*.

V *"The Ballad of Reading Gaol"*

Writing to William Roger Paton in early August of 1897, Oscar Wilde mentioned a new long poem he had written in "a new style . . . full of actuality and life in its directness of message and meaning" (*Letters*, pp. 269-630). "The Ballad of Reading Gaol" did indeed represent for Wilde a new departure from his poetic efforts of the past, for the raw materials from which it was created came from his direct experiences with prison life.

In the early summer of 1896 Wilde noticed a new prisoner about thirty years of age in the prison yard. He was dressed in "a suit of shabby grey" as he had not received regular prison clothes because he was a "remand" prisoner.[31] Wilde discovered that this prisoner was a trooper in the Royal Horse Guards named Charles Thomas Wooldridge, who had been charged with the murder of his twenty-three-year-old wife. Wooldridge was said to have "cut his wife's throat in a very determined manner, she having excited his jealousy, and (so far as the evidence went) greatly annoyed him."[32] Wooldridge was sentenced by Mr. Justice Hawkins at the Berkshire Assizes on June 17, hanged three weeks later, and buried in quicklime outside the prison walls. For a man such as Wilde, who for much of his lifetime had lived and preached the pursuit of the beautiful and the artificial, the forced confrontation with one of the harshest realities of prison life must have been indeed traumatic. What in Pater's Aestheticism could prepare him for so concrete an illustration of "man's inhumanity to man?"

The idea for the "Ballad" had occurred to him while in prison. After Wilde was released May 19, 1897, he went to Berneval, France, with friends and began work on this poem. Wilde seems to have had much difficulty with the "Ballad" if the great number of references to it in his correspondence are any indication. On August 24 he wrote to Leonard Smithers that he wanted to see his poem typewritten for "I am sick of my manuscript" (*Letters*, p. 635). Yet by September 4 he wrote to Robert Ross explaining that he had still not finished his poem (*Letters*, p. 638). Finally, on Thursday, October 14, he wrote from Naples, where he was living with Lord Alfred Douglas, that his work was finished: "I have finished the great poem—six hundred lines now. I hope it will make a good effect. I like much of it myself. Much is, I feel, for a harsher instrument than the languorous flute *I* love" (*Letters*, p. 656). The reasons for Wilde's difficulties no doubt lay in his employment of a new idiom. He had set aside the blends of Impressionism and Expressionism[33] of such poems as "Impression du Matin," "The Harlot's House," and the "Sphinx" and employed for the first time a poetic medium that seemed to communicate experience directly.

After the poem was completed Wilde's thoughts turned to the question of a publisher. No reputable publisher was likely to risk issuing anything of Oscar Wilde's. John Lane, who had published most of his earlier works, now would have nothing to do with anything of Wilde's. According to Vincent O'Sullivan, Robert Ross suggested Leonard Smithers, an unusual publisher and man, who had boasted that he would "publish anything that the others are afraid of."[34] Although he sold pornography on the side, he also published poets like Ernest Dowson and Vincent O'Sullivan and artists like Max Beerbohm and Aubrey Beardsley.

"The Ballad of Reading Gaol" was finally published February 13, 1898. The first edition of eight hundred copies and a limited printing of thirty copies on Japanese vellum appeared without the author's name, only his cell number at Reading—C.3.3.[35] There was a dedication to "C. T. W. Sometime Trooper of the Royal Horse Guards" and an additional dedication to Ross which Smithers cancelled.[36] Seven authorized editions were printed, the last bearing Oscar Wilde's name in parentheses after C.3.3. Although the sixth edition appeared in May 1898 within only three months, only a thousand or so copies were printed for each edition[37] so that Wilde complained to Ross about Smither's judgment: "I fear he has missed a popular 'rush.' He is so fond of 'suppressed' books that he suppresses his own" (Letters, p. 705).

"The Ballad of Reading Gaol" consists of 654 lines arranged into 109 six-line stanzas. By adding two extra lines to the conventional ballad form, Wilde achieved the effect either of refrain or reflective commentary. The poem is further arranged into six "cantos" (Wilde's term) that are, with the exception of the last, further arranged into stanza groupings usually separated by asterisks.

The first canto provides the reader with a look at the condemned man from the point of view first of the prison community as embodied in the voice of the speaker:

> I walked, with other souls in pain,
>   Within another ring,
> And was wondering if the man had done
>   A great or little thing,
> When a voice behind me whispered low,
>   "That fellow's got to swing." (ll. 19-24)

The second section of the first canto shifts to a reflection upon the crimes of mankind in general:

> Yet each man kills the thing he loves,
>   By each let this be heard,

> Some do it with a bitter look,
>   Some with a flattering word,
> The coward does it with a kiss,
>   The brave man with a sword! (ll. 37-42)

The third section affirms the bond that all men have with the condemned man by revealing in hypnotic, repetitive lines what the common run of mankind does not suffer for its crimes: "He does not sit with silent men/Who watch him night and day . . . . "/He does not wake at dawn to see/Dread figures throng his room" (ll. 61-62, 67-68).

The second canto begins with a description of the condemned man's last hungry look at the world around him. But the primary emphasis is upon the feeling of identification with his suffering that the other prisoners felt. In the third canto, which recounts the days preceding the execution, the sense of kinship with the prisoner reaches its greatest intensity. Most significant is the intense sense of shared guilt:

> Alas! it is a fearful thing
>   To feel another's guilt!
> For, right within, the sword of Sin
>   Pierced to its poisoned hilt,
> And as molten lead were the tears we shed
>   For the blood we had not spilt. (ll. 265-270)

The last section of this canto describes the psychological effects upon the prisoners as they waited for the dawn of the day of execution. The stark yet suggestive details reveal the extent to which Wilde has discarded the vague Impressionism of his earlier style:

> At last I saw the shadowed bars,
>   Like a lattice wrought in lead,
> Move right across the whitewashed wall
>   That faced my three-plank bed,
> And I knew that somewhere in the world
>   God's dreadful dawn was red. (ll. 337-342)

Canto four describes the state of mind after the execution. The prisoners seem to adopt the demeanor of the condemned man: "I never saw sad men who looked/With such a wistful eve/Upon that little tent of blue/We prisoners called the sky" (ll. 415-420). At this point Wilde most strikingly reveals his central theme—that all men share in a collective guilt for their acquiesence in such crimes:

> But there were those amongst us all
> Who walked with downcast head,
> And knew that, had each got his due,
> They should have died instead:
> He had but killed a thing that lived,
> Whilst they had killed the dead.
> For he who sins a second time ˙
> Wakes a dead soul to pain,
> And draws it from its spotted shroud,
> And makes it bleed again,
> And makes it bleed great gouts of blood,
> And makes it bleed in vain! (ll. 421-432)

The Christian imagery is further intensified by the speaker's suggestion that "God's kindly earth/Is kindlier than men know,/And the red rose would but blow more red,/The white rose whiter blow" (ll. 477-480). The executed man has become a sacrificial figure, a Christ whose death makes men's lives meaningful.

To Robert Ross, who had suggested that Wilde end the poem after the fourth canto, Wilde had this reply: "You are quite right in saying that the poem should end at 'outcasts always mourn,' but the propaganda, which I desire to make, begins there" (*Letters*, p. 661). For example, the third stanza reveals Wilde's distress at the cruelty of the legal system and its prisons:

> This too I know—and wise it were
> If each could know the same—
> That every prison that men build
> Is built with bricks of shame,
> And bound with bars lest Christ should see
> How men their brothers maim. (ll. 547-552)

The final three sections of canto five describe in powerful terms the fact that "It is only what is good in Man/That wastes and withers there" (ll. 561-562).

The sixth canto consists of only eighteen lines. Although Christ is mentioned, the prevailing theme of universal culpability is muted.

The events are distanced by a shift to an impersonal, even official, poetic voice that opens the canto with an epitaph-like series of lines:

> In Reading Gaol by Reading Town
> There is a pit of shame,
> And in it lies a wretched man
> Eaten by teeth of flame,
> In a burning winding-sheet he lies,
> And his grave has got no name. (ll. 637-642)

The poem ends with a variation of one of the earliest stanzas:

> And all men kill the thing they love,
> By all let this be heard,
> Some do it with a bitter look,
> Some with a flattering word,
> The coward does it with a kiss,
> The brave man with a sword! (ll. 649-654)

The poem in general is constructed as a series of sharply etched tableaux that are visualized by a never-individualized first person narrator who sometimes speaks as a single participant and sometimes as the prisoners' collective voice. Only rarely, and then only dimly, can the early Wildean poetic voice be heard. Wilde is not attempting in the Paterian sense to see the object (or experience) by knowing his own impression as it really is, but to communicate experience and its effects in terms of those who suffer man's institutionalized cruelties. To achieve this purpose, Wilde employs the simple, stark details of prison experience and uses them expressionistically and symbolically. In a letter to Frank Harris he expressed his clear awareness that his poetic method violated his own artistic principles: "I, of course, feel that the poem is autobiographical and that *real* experiences are alien things that should never influence one, but it was wrung out of me, a cry of pain, the cry of Marsyas, not the song of Apollo" (*Letters*, p. 708). That Wilde was conscious of working with new materials, with new principles, is made clear by his response to Ross's criticism of his poem:

> The difficulty is that the objects in prison have no shape or form. To take an example: the shed in which people are hanged is a little shed with a glass roof, like a photographer's studio on the sands at Margate. For eighteen

months I thought it *was* the studio for photographing prisoners. There is no adjective to describe it. I call it "hideous" because it became so to me after I knew its use. In itself it is a wooden, oblong, narrow shed with a glass roof.

A cell again may be described *psychologically*, with reference to its effect on the soul: in itself it can only be described as "whitewashed" or "dimly-lit." It has no shape. no contents. It does not exist from the point of view of form or colour. (*Letters*, pp. 654-655)

What Wilde describes in his letter is the artistic process by which the concreteness of the prisoner's environment is made to reflect the prisoner's heightened sensibility and his existential state. Actually, the absence of rich details and forms probably worked to Wilde's advantage. Such details as a shadow, the colors gray, white, and red, and a moving pattern across a blank wall are sufficient materials for the poet as Wilde's stanza reveals:

> At last I saw the shadowed bars,
>   Like a lattice wrought in lead
> Move right across the whitewashed wall
>   That faced my three-plank bed,
> And I knew that somewhere in the world
>   God's dreadful dawn was red. (ll. 337-342)

This is no longer Victorian poetry. Wilde had been reading Housman's *A Shropshire Lad* (1896); and its influence can be felt in Wilde's poem.[38] It is hard to disagree with Roditi who argues that ". . . many of its thoughts and sentiments are typical of a new poetry that is no longer Victorian and to whose flowering Wilde had at that time contributed as much as Housman."[39] It seems clear, as Buckley suggests, that only in "The Ballad of Reading Gaol" did Wilde achieve the intensity, self-effacement, and high seriousness necessary to produce the "one beautiful work of art of which he dreamed."[40] What makes this poetry of a new sort is not its subject matter, sentiments, or high seriousness but its affinities with the poetic techniques of Thomas Hardy and A. E. Housman.

CHAPTER 3

The Stories

O SCAR Wilde loved to tell stories. Hesketh Pearson, Wilde's
biographer, tells of how dozens of tales would occur to him
during the course of conversations, over a drink at parties, while
watching a painter at work, or at any odd time.[1] But the effort to
write them down was irksome to Wilde so that his three volumes of
short stories represent only a sampling of his talent. That he had a
genius for storytelling is unquestioned. That Wilde was pleased with
his tales, especially the fairy tales, is clear from his letters; but there
is little evidence that he felt they would represent a major portion of
his reputation as a writer.[2] Yet to millions of children and adults for
close to a century such titles as "The Happy Prince," "The Canterville Ghost," and "The Selfish Giant" bring a light of recognition
that few of Wilde's other works can do. Still, in spite of their enduring popularity, Wilde's short stories and fairy tales have not drawn
much critical attention. This neglect has been unfortunate, for the
tales are interesting, not only as objects of literary study, but for the
light they shed on Wilde's basic literary strategies.

Many of the stories possess the ornate stylistic embellishments
found in the larger, more consciously artistic works such as *Salome*
or *The Picture of Dorian Gray*. In "The Happy Prince," for example,
the reader will recognize characteristic Wildean touches in the swallow's descriptions of his exotic Egyptian homeland. "The Fisherman
and His Soul" possesses the same lengthy catalogues of exotic
jewels, precious metals, sounds, textures, and smells that Wilde so
often included in his more self-consciously artistic works. Often
Wilde's descriptions are rendered so impressionistically, as in "Lord
Arthur Savile's Crime" or "The Young King," that they remind the
reader of Whistler's painting technique. In several of these tales,
most noticeably "The Birthday of the Infanta," these descriptions
are more effectively integrated into the narrative than they are in
such works as *Salome* or *The Picture of Dorian Gray*.

The dandiacal hero, so common in Wilde's other works, also appears in the stories. "Lord Arthur Savile's Crime," for example, has a protagonist who strongly anticipates Dorian Gray, especially in the nature of his responses to both beauty and ugliness. Even "The Remarkable Rocket," a story that Pater liked,[3] has a dandiacal protagonist. Accompanying this common Wildean figure is the usual heavy dose of paradoxical Wildean wit. "The Canterville Ghost," which has a supernatural dandy, and "Lord Arthur Savile's Crime" are most noteworthy in this respect.

The themes and subject matter of Wilde's stories are essentially the same as those of his other works. Wilde's deep concern with social issues is strikingly evident in such stories as "The Happy Prince," "The Birthday of the Infanta," and "The Star-Child." The lack of understanding or sympathy between the sensitive artistic soul and the unfeeling Philistine majority, a common theme in Wilde's other works, is prominent also in "The Devoted Friend," "The Happy Prince," and "The Nightingale and the Rose." There is an underlying sense in many of the stories, especially "The Star-Child," "The Birthday of the Infanta," and "The Devoted Friend," of the cruelty of man's world as opposed to that of Nature. The common Wildean theme of the superiority of the artificial to the natural, so highly developed in such critical works as "The Critic as Artist," appears in "Lord Arthur Savile's Crime," "The Young King," and "The Birthday of the Infanta." Some critics have been struck by Wilde's fascination with the Christ or scapegoat figure in the tales.[4] Such Christlike sufferers appear in "The Happy Prince," "The Selfish Giant," "The Star-Child," and "The Nightingale and the Rose." Accompanying the Christlike protagonist in such stories are the parallel themes of guilt, suffering, and love.

I   Lord Arthur Savile's Crime and Other Stories

Wilde first tried his hand at short fiction when he was editing *The Woman's World* and reviewing for the *Pall Mall Gazette*. He had an apparently inexhaustible store of tales which he loved to tell as much as his friends loved to hear them.[5] "The Canterville Ghost: A Hylo-Idealistic Romance," the first of Wilde's short tales, appeared in two parts in *The Court and Society Review* in February and March of 1887. "Lord Arthur Savile's Crime: A Study of Duty" appeared in *The Court and Society Review* on May 11, 18, and 25, 1887. "The Sphinx Without a Secret: An Etching," appeared in *The*

World on May 25, 1887, entitled "Lady Alroy." "The Model Millionaire: A Note of Admiration" first appeared in *The World* on June
22, 1887. These stories were gathered together and published under
the title *Lord Arthur Savile's Crime and Other Stories* in July of
1891.

The title story of Wilde's volume tells of young Lord Arthur
Savile's strange encounter with a chiromantist at a fashionable society reception. In a private meeting with Mr. Podgers, the
chiromantist, Lord Savile learned with horror that murder was written in his palm. After a night of wandering through the city in
despair, he realized he could not marry his beloved Sybil Merton
until he had committed the murder. He decided to murder his
second cousin on his mother's side, dear old Lady Clementina. But,
unfortunately, though he had bought an elaborate poison disguised
as candy, the old lady happened to die of natural causes. Again
delaying his marriage he bought an exploding clock in order to blow
up his uncle, the Dean of Chichester. When the newspaper failed to
report an explosion, he was distressed. He later learned that when
the clock had emitted a little puff of smoke as it struck noon, it had
merely amused everyone highly. Saddened, he went walking in the
evening along the Thames. As he approached Cleopatra's Needle,
he saw Mr. Podgers leaning over the parapet. Suddenly a brilliant
idea occurred to him. He seized Mr. Podgers by the knees and
threw him into the Thames. The next day the newspapers reported
the suicide of a chiromantist. Lord Savile and Sybil were married in
three weeks. Several years later Lady Windermere asked Sybil
whether she remembered that horrid impostor, Mr. Podgers. Sybil
replied that she must not say anything against chiromantists for
Arthur was a firm believer. When Lady Windermere asked Arthur
the reason for such a belief, he replied "Because I owe to it all the
happiness of my life."

The story contains the earliest appearance in Wilde's work, except for Prince Paul Maraloffski in *Vera*, of the dandy figure. Early
in the story the reader learns that Lord Arthur has "lived the delicate and luxurious life of a young man of birth and fortune, a life
exquisite in its freedom from sordid care, its beautiful boyish in-
souciance; and now for the first time he had become conscious of the
terrible mystery of Destiny, of the awful meaning of Doom" ("Lord
Arthur Savile's Crime," p. 173). Like the later Dorian Gray, Lord
Savile is intensely responsive to beauty and sadly aware of secret
sins unguessed by ordinary people:

As he strolled home towards Belgrave Square, he met the great waggons on their way to Covent Garden. The white-smocked carters, with their pleasant sunburnt faces and coarse curly hair, strode sturdily on, cracking their whips, and calling out now and then to each other; on the back of a huge grey horse, the leader of a jangling team, sat a chubby boy, with a bunch of primroses in his battered hat, keeping tight hold of the mane with his little hands, and laughing; and the great piles of vegetables looked like masses of jade against the morning sky, like masses of green jade against the pink petals of some marvelous rose. Lord Arthur felt curiously affected, he could not tell why. There was something in the dawn's delicate loveliness that seemed to him inexpressibly pathetic, and he thought of all the days that break in beauty,and that set in storm. These rustics, too, with their rough, good-humoured voices, and their nonchalant ways, what a strange London they saw! A London free from the sin of night and the smoke of day, a pallid, ghost-like city, a desolate town of tombs! He wondered what they thought of it, and whether they knew anything of its splendour and its shame, of its fierce, fiery-coloured joys, and its horrible hunger, of all it makes and mars from morn to eve. ("Lord Arthur Savile's Crime," pp. 176-177)

This passage might have been taken from *Dorian Gray*, for the note of *fin-de-siècle* world-weariness, the emphasis upon sensuous detail, the juxtaposition of beauty against the chaos and clamor of existence, and the sense of beauty's restorative power are all present.

Although many of the critical ideas embodied in *Dorian Gray* are suggested by these detectable qualities, nowhere is any conscious effort made to create a coherent aesthetic. The delicate descriptions of dawn in Piccadilly or the description of the night from the Thames Embankment—"The moon peered thröugh a mane of tawny clouds, as if it were a lion's eye, and innumerable stars spangled the hollow vault, like gold dust powdered on a purple dome" ("Lord Arthur Savile's Crime," p. 189)—are striking and Whistlerian, but they are only fictional embellishments, and the tone they achieve frequently conflicts with that created by Wilde's satire and humor.

"The Sphinx Without a Secret," Wilde's second story, is brief and entertaining but sheds little light on the development of Oscar Wilde's art except for the traces it provides of the Wildean dandy and the witty style he was to employ with such effectiveness in later works. The story begins with the dandiacal narrator commenting with *fin-de-siècle* weariness about life: "One afternoon I was sitting outside the Café de la Paix, watching the splendour and shabbiness of Parisian life, and wondering over my vermouth at the strange panorama of pride and poverty that was passing before me, when I heard some one call my name" ("The Sphinx Without a Secret," p. 215). The narrator in this early story possesses the detachment that Lord Henry Wotton recognizes as essential to an aesthetically successful life. When our narrator examines the photograph of the beautiful woman of mystery, his impression is appropriately subtle: "It seemed to me the face of some one who had a secret, but whether that secret was good or evil I could not say. Its beauty was a beauty moulded out of many mysteries—the beauty, in fact, which is psychological, not plastic—and the faint smile that just played across the lips was far too subtle to be really sweet" ("The Sphinx Without a Secret," pp. 215-216). The echo of Pater is unmistakable and suggests the early development of the character Wilde was later to create so brilliantly in *Dorian Gray* and the society comedies.

"The Canterville Ghost: A Hylo-Idealistic Romance," Wilde's third story, is about Hiram B. Otis, the American minister, and his family who buy Canterville Chase, a mansion haunted since 1584. But the Otis family, which included Washington, the eldest son, Virginia, a lovely girl of fifteen, and the twin boys, did not believe in ghosts and soon arranged to move in. A series of strange occurrences such as disappearing bloodstains and ghostly visitations soon took place. But each occurrence not only failed to frighten the practical-minded Otises but resulted in the humiliation of the ghost. He vowed vengeance but time after time his efforts to frighten the Otises were thwarted by the pranks of the children and the patent nostrums of the adults. One day when Virginia discovered the ghost sitting sadly by a window, she learned that the ghost had had no rest for three hundred years. The old ghost then told her of the prophecy that someone must weep for his sins because he had no tears and pray with him for his soul because he had no faith. He told her that she could open the Portals of Death's house for love is always with her and love is stronger than death. She agreed to help and disappeared with him through the wainscoting into a cavern-like passage. At midnight, accompanied by a peal of thunder and unearthly music, a panel in the wall opened. Virginia stepped out with a casket of jewels and the news that the old ghost was now dead. Several years later when Virginia's husband Cecil asked what had happened when she was locked up with the ghost, she only revealed that she owed him a great deal, for "He made me see what Life is, and what Death signifies, and why Love is stronger than both."

"The Canterville Ghost" is an obvious satirization of the manners and tastes of Americans. Wilde no doubt had derived many of these impressions from his American tours. However, the satire is never indicative of real hostility toward Americans. The brashness, cockiness, and depressing practicality of the Otises serve only as matter for Wilde's comic purposes. His burlesquing of the trappings of the macabre story provides another means by which he produces comic effect. The ghost takes a kind of dandiacal pride in the rich variety of frightening appearances he has created throughout the centuries. The ghost comically savors his disguises as "Red Ruben, or the Strangled Babe" or "Gaunt Gibeon, the Blood-Sucker of Bexley Moor" or "Jonas the Graveless, or the Corpse-Snatcher of Chertsey Barn." However, Wilde's ghost is a bungler. His greatest disappointment occurred when he put on his suit of armor for "He had hoped that even modern Americans would be thrilled by the sight of a Spectre in Armour, if for no more sensible reason, at least out of respect for their national poet Longfellow, over whose graceful and attractive poetry he himself had whiled away many a weary hour when the Cantervilles were up in town." However, when the ghost donned his armor, he was overpowered by its weight and fell, barking both shins. The ghost never succeeds at frightening the Otises. He falls victim to the harassment of trip wires, pea shooters, and falling buckets of water instigated by the Otis children.

The story possesses a conventionally melodramatic plot as Wilde obviously intended. A variety of devices from the Gothic terror tale are included such as guilty ghosts, prophecies, curses, and mysterious revelations, but all these are deliberately undercut by comic devices. Thus, it is possible to disagree with Roditis' judgment that "Instead of clothing his plot in an appropriate atmosphere, Wilde relies . . . on stock witticisms and heavy satire on the bad tastes and manners and prejudices of Americans. . . ."[6] Wilde actually incorporates much that in typical Gothic fiction would be productive of atmosphere. But the intrusion of such comic matter is Wilde's means of undercutting this for comic effect. Actually, the story is weakened, as Pearson suggests, by its shift from social satire to pure burlesque to romantic sentiment.[7]

The last tale in Wilde's volume of short stories is entitled "A Model Millionaire: A Note of Admiration" and tells the story of Hughie Erskine, who possessed every accomplishment except that of making money. He was a delightfully ineffectual young man with a perfect profile and no profession. He wanted to marry Laura Merton but her father would not hear of any engagement until he had ten thousand pounds. One morning Hugh dropped in to see his friend Alan Trevor, the painter. Hughie was so affected by the pitiful appearance of the beggar Alan was painting that he gave him a sovereign. Later, much to his chagrin, he discovered from his friend that the beggar was Baron Hausberg, one of the richest men in Europe. He also learned that the Baron had been much amused by the incident. The next day an old gentleman delivered an envelope from Baron Hausberg containing a check for ten thousand pounds with the following note: "A wedding present to Hugh Erskine and Laura Merton from an old beggar." At the wedding breakfast Baron Hausberg made a speech and Alan remarked that "Millionaire models are rare enough; but, by jove, model millionaires are rarer still!"

Although we might concur with Arthur Ransome's judgment that "A Model Millionaire" was an "empty little thing,"[8] we would have to agree that it does reveal Wilde's delightful gifts as a storyteller. Moreover, we would no doubt find Wilde's tale wanting if we attempted to compare it, as Edouard Roditi does, with so complex a work as Henry James' "The Real Thing."[9] But the story does possess a generous portion of Wildean wit. The relationship between the ingenuous Hughie and that of Alan Trevor reminds us a little of the friendship of Dorian Gray and Basil Hallward except that Alan Trevor in this case gets the few dandiacal lines: "Men who are dandies and women who are darlings rule the world, at least they should do so." Beyond the wit and the few hints at later themes, Wilde seems concerned primarily with his ability to entertain and to charm.

II The Happy Prince and Other Tales

Oscar Wilde published *The Happy Prince and Other Tales* in May 1888. This volume of fairy tales and, to a lesser extent, *A House of Pomegranates* constitute two of Wilde's significant achievements as a prose writer if enduring popularity is any criterion. Wilde himself called them ". . . studies in prose, put for Romance's sake into a fanciful form: meant partly for children, and partly for those who have kept the childlike faculties of wonder and joy, and who find in simplicity a subtle strangeness" (*Letters*, p. 219). It seems clear that Wilde felt he was creating something that fulfilled his own ideas of art. Writing to Amelie Rives Chanler, he said that his fairy tales were "an attempt to mirror modern life in a form remote from reality—to deal with modern problems in a mode that is ideal and not imitative . . . they are of course, slight and fanciful, and written, not for children, but for childlike people from eighteen to eighty!" (*Letters*, p. 237)

Wilde's tales, illustrated by Walter Crane and Jacob Hood, were well received by the critics. The *Athenaeum* said they were "not unworthy to compare with Hans Andersen, and it is not easy to give higher praise than this."[10] The *Saturday Review* was pleased with Wilde's tales but felt they differed from Andersen's in the quality of satire they possessed, a quality designed to please adult readers.[11] Walter Pater, Wilde's former teacher at Oxford, delighted him with these words of praise: ". . . I hardly know whether to admire more the wise wit of The Wonderful [Remarkable] Rocket, or the beauty and tenderness of The Selfish Giant: the latter certainly is perfect in its kind. Your genuine 'little poems in prose,' those at the top of pages 10 and 14, for instance, are gems, and the whole, too brief, book abounds with delicate touches and pure English" (*Letters*, p. 219n).

The title story of the volume is about the statue of the Happy Prince, which stood high above the city on a tall column: "He was gilded all over with thin leaves of fine gold, for eyes he had two bright sapphires, and a large red ruby glowed on his sword-hilt." One day a little swallow who had delayed his winter trip to Egypt because he had fallen in love with a reed stopped to rest on the column. After several drops of water had fallen upon him, he looked up and saw that the statue was weeping. The swallow asked him why he was weeping, and the Happy Prince replied that until he had died and been placed high above the city he did not know of the misery in the world. The statue then asked the swallow to take the ruby out of his sword-hilt and give it to a poor woman whose little boy was sick with a fever. At the Prince's request the swallow agreed to remain one night longer and, although it was cold, felt a little warmer after his task. The next day the swallow stayed to deliver one of the Prince's sapphire eyes to a poor writer who was so cold he could no longer write his play. The third day he took the last sapphire to a little match girl who had lost her matches. The little swallow decided to stay with the now-blind statue and tell him stories of strange marvels he had seen. But the prince told him that the suffering of man was more marvelous still and asked him to pick off the gold leaf and give it to the poor. The swallow did this and the poor were happy. But the cold winter had come and the little swallow had just enough strength left to kiss the Happy Prince and die. At that moment the leaden heart of the statue broke in two. When the mayor and the town councillors saw how shabby the statue had become, they had it pulled down and melted. Because the heart would not melt, they threw it on the dustheap where the swallow was lying. God then asked one of his angels to bring him the two most precious things in the city. The angel brought the leaden heart and the little body of the bird. God decreed that "in my garden of Paradise this little bird shall sing for evermore, and in my city of gold the Happy Prince shall praise me."

Wilde thought that "The Happy Prince" was the best of the tales. He said that his story was "an attempt to treat a tragic modern problem in a form that aims at delicacy and imaginative treatment: it is a reaction against the purely imitative character of modern art. . . ." (*Letters*, p. 220). Wilde's point is well taken for at least one of the striking qualities of this tale, as well as others, lies in the rhythmical, highly ornamental prose Wilde uses to sharply illuminate his scenes. The effect in some cases is a rich, sensuous prose-poetry: "My friends are flying up and down the Nile, and talking to the large lotus-flowers. Soon they will go to sleep in the tomb of the great King. The King is there himself in his painted coffin. He is wrapped in yellow linen, and embalmed with spices. Round his neck is a chain of pale green jade, and his hands are like withered leaves" ("Happy Prince," p. 287). In other passages the effect is stark but no less visually suggestive: "He flew into dark lanes, and saw the white faces of starving children looking out listlessly at the black streets" (p. 290). On other occasions Wilde's language modulates into the highly ornate adjectival embroidery characteristic of much of the poetry, *Dorian Gray*, and the poetic drama:

All the next day he sat on the Prince's shoulder, and told him stories of what he had seen in strange lands. He told him of the red ibises, who stand in long rows on the banks of the Nile, and catch goldfish in their beaks; of the Sphinx, who is as old as the world itself, and lives in the desert, and knows everything; of the merchants, who walk slowly by the side of their camels and carry amber beads in their hands; of the King of the Mountains of the Moon, who is as black as ebony, and worships a large crystal; of the great green snake that sleeps in a palm-tree, and has twenty priests to feed it with honey-cakes; and of the pygmies who sail over a big lake on large flat leaves, and are always at war with the butterflies. ("Happy Prince," pp. 289-290)

The effect of such prose and what can best be described as the
Biblical tone is to distance the reader from the social realities Wilde
is clearly distressed by and force the reader to experience the work
first as art. As Wilde argued in "The Critic as Artist," "The real artist
is he who proceeds, not from feeling to form, but from form to
thought and passion" ("Critic as Artist," II, p. 398).

An aspect of the structure of the story and a primary means of
intensifying the reader's anxious involvement are the refrainlike
commands of the Happy Prince: "Swallow, Swallow, little Swallow . . . will you not stay with me one night longer?" followed usually by "Swallow, Swallow, little Swallow . . . do as I command
you." Combined with the highly rhythmic language these refrains
have an incremental effect that is central to the tale's effectiveness.

"The Nightingale and the Rose" is a story about a nightingale who
one day overheard a young student lamenting that his life was
wretched for the lack of a red rose. "Here at last is a true lover," said
the nightingale when she saw his beauty and passion. When she
overheard him murmur that his love would not dance with him at
the ball tomorrow unless he brought her a red rose, she thought
about the mystery of love. Then suddenly she flew away to find a red
rose. She went to several rose trees but found only white and yellow
roses. A third rose tree told her that his roses were red but that
winter had chilled his veins and he would have no roses that year.
When the nightingale implored the rose tree for just one red rose,
the Rose Tree told her of one terrible way to get one. The nightingale "must build it out of music by moonlight and stain it with her
own heart's blood by singing to the tree with her breast against a
thorn." The bird thought that death was a great price to pay for a red
rose yet Love was better than Life. The oak tree, who loved the
nightingale, asked her to sing one last song. When the nightingale
had finished, the student, who had heard the song, complained that
it was a pity that the nightingale was all style and no sincereity. All
night long the little nightingale sang with the thorn against her
breast while the rose slowly grew. When it was finished, the little
bird was dead. At noon the student opened his window and found
the beautiful red rose. He quickly carried the flower to his loved one
and reminded her of her promise. But the girl told him that it would
not go with her dress and, besides, the chamberlain's nephew was
sending her some real jewels, and everybody knows that jewels are
more costly than flowers. The student called the girl ungrateful and

threw the rose into the street. He then decided that love was silly and that he would go back to philosophy and metaphysics.

Although Wilde felt "The Happy Prince" was the best story in his volume, he considered "The Nightingale and the Rose" the "most elaborate" (*Letters*, p. 220). He no doubt admired the complexity created by the ironic contrast between the student's underevaluation of the nightingale's song and the nightingale's overevaluation of the student's sincerity. When the nightingale sings one last song to the oak tree that loved her, the student, who "only knew the things that are written down in books," reveals himself as a shallow critic: "She has form . . . that cannot be denied to her; but has she got feeling? I am afraid not. In fact, she is like most artists; she is all style without any sincerity. She would not sacrifice herself for others. She thinks merely of music, and everybody knows that the arts are selfish. Still, it must be admitted that she has some beautiful notes in her voice. What a pity it is that they do not mean anything, or do any practical good!" ("The Nightingale and the Rose," p. 294) The nightingale, the true artist, is about to sing its heart's blood away for the student, the true Philistine. For Oscar Wilde life could provide no greater irony nor deeper tragedy. The student was not one of "the elect to whom beautiful things mean only Beauty" (*The Picture of Dorian Gray*, p. 17). Thus, Wilde succeeds at incorporating several of the main elements of his artistic credo in this story.

Other characteristic elements add to the richness of the story's fabric. The student is described in conventional Wildean terms: "His hair is dark as the hyacinth-blossom, and his lips are red as the rose of his desire; but passion has made his face like pale ivory, and sorrow has set her seal upon his brow" ("The Nightingale and the Rose," p. 292). In addition, the story is filled with the highly ornate passages Wilde so loved: "Then she gave one last burst of music. The white moon heard it, and she forgot the dawn, and lingered on in the sky. The red rose heard it, and it trembled all over with ecstasy, and opened its petals to the cold morning air. Echo bore it to her purple cavern in the hills, and woke the sleeping shepherds from their dreams. It floated through the reeds of the river, and they carried its message to the sea." ("The Nightingale and the Rose," p. 295) The very artificiality of Wilde's style and the distancing effect it creates is the source of a portion of Wilde's success with the fairy tale.

"The Selfish Giant," Wilde's third tale, tells of a giant who had a beautiful garden that the children loved to play in after school. One day the giant came back after having been away for seven years. When he saw the children playing in his garden, he became angry and chased them away. The selfish giant then erected a sign warning that trespassers would be prosecuted. When spring came all the countryside became green and flowery except the giant's garden. The flowers and the trees did not want to bloom because there were no children. The birds did not care to sing. Then the Snow and the Frost invited the North Wind and the Hail to stay with them in the cold garden all the year round. One morning the giant awakened to the sound of a bird singing beautifully. He looked out his window and saw a child sitting in every tree. The trees were so glad to have the children back that they were blossoming everywhere except in one corner where a little boy too small to climb his tree stood crying. The giant's heart melted as he realized how selfish he had been. All the children except the little boy ran away when he came out into the garden. But they returned when they saw the giant help the boy into the tree. Every afternoon from that time on the children played in the garden, but the giant never saw the little boy again. One day, years later when he was very old, the giant looked out and saw a beautiful tree in the corner of his garden with the boy standing beside it. With great joy he ran into the garden but became angry when he saw nail wounds on the boy's hands and feet. The giant vowed to slay the person who had hurt him, but the boy replied that those were the wounds of love. The giant knelt and the little boy smiled and said, "You let me play once in your garden, today you shall come with me to my garden, which is Paradise." The children later found the giant lying dead under the blossoming tree.

In many of Wilde's fairy tales the motifs of suffering and redemption through love appear as consistent threads. A variety of writers have remarked upon the fascination Wilde seemed to have had throughout his life for Christianity and especially the figure of Christ.[12] This interest revealed itself in a wide spectrum of his works, most notably *Vera*, *Salome*, "De Profundis," "The Ballad of Reading Gaol," and, of course, the fairy tales. This Christ motif permeates the texture of "The Selfish Giant" most visibly. The little boy whom the giant had helped into the tree long ago finally returns with the marks of crucifixion on his hands and feet and a message of love.

The Christian parallels in "The Selfish Giant" are clear-cut, but

Wilde gives his tale a further mythic dimension by embodying his basic Christian themes in images of both a procreant and a desiccated natural world. The garden, a beautiful verdant paradise, becomes through the giant's selfishness or lack of love a barren wasteland torn by cold winds, hail, and snow. Only by the giant's change of heart or act of love does the wasteland become a fertile garden again. The giant's reward, of course, is an eternity in Christ's garden.

"The Devoted Friend" is a story told by a linnet to a water rat. One day a mother duck, trying to teach her inattentive children how to stand on their heads in the water, was told by a water rat that such disobedient children deserved to be drowned. When the mother defended her brood, the water rat replied that although he knew nothing of the feelings of parents, he felt friendship was much nobler than love. At that point a nearby green linnet told him the story of honest little Hans who had as his devoted friend big Hugh the Miller. Hans was such a devoted friend that he never refused his friend anything, but the Miller never gave him anything in return except noble ideas about friendship. One night the Miller asked Hans to get a doctor for his injured son. Hans agreed to go even when the Miller refused to lend his lantern. Hans struggled through the dreadful storm and notified the doctor, but on the way back in the darkness he fell into a pond and was drowned. The Miller was the chief mourner at his funeral but only complained of the way one must suffer for being overly generous. When the linnet was finished, the water rat was angry at learning that this was a story with a moral. The duck told the linnet that telling stories with morals was a dangerous thing to do. The green linnet agreed.

"The Devoted Friend" is the only one of Wilde's stories that possesses a "moral" in the conventional sense. In fact, there are two morals. The first is that mere high-sounding praise of friendship without corresponding deeds is wrong, just as a foolish acquiescence to the unreasonable demands of friendship is wrong. Yet it is tempting to supply an additional level of meaning to the tale beyond that of the moral tale. In the character of Hugh the Miller we have an exemplar of what Wilde felt was the unfortunate modern belief that considerations of human kindness and feeling have no place in economic affairs. Wilde is also attacking what he saw as the tendency of the wealthy and privileged classes to justify their own indifference and selfishness by specious economic and moral rationalizations. The social consciousness that Wilde was to reveal in such later works as "The Soul of Man Under Socialism," "De Profundis," and "The Ballad of Reading Gaol" is much in evidence in this story.

The final story in *The Happy Prince and Other Tales* is "The Remarkable Rocket." This tale takes place on the day the King's son is to marry a beautiful Russian princess. As a finale a great fireworks display was to be held. When all the fireworks were put in their places, they began to talk with each other. A little squib, a Roman Candle, a Catherine Wheel, and other fireworks began to argue about the world and romance. They were interrupted by a supercilious-looking rocket tied to a long stick who began to tell them of his distinction as a rocket. He was descended from renowned parents who had made brilliant public appearances. After annoying the other fireworks with such self-adulation, the supercilious rocket began to weep at an imaginary misfortune. When the rocket display began, all the other fireworks made a magnificent display. But the proud rocket had wept himself into such a damp state that he failed to ignite. But the rocket thought he was being held in reserve for a special occasion. When the workman called him a "bad rocket" and threw him into a ditch, he insisted that they must have said "Grand Rocket" for the words sounded so much alike. He continued to speak in his proud way to a frog, a dragonfly, and a duck he encountered in the ditch. Finally, some young boys saw an "old stick," which the rocket interpreted as "Gold Stick," and pulled the rocket from the mud. The rocket was delighted when the boys threw him into their cooking fire for he thought they were setting him off in broad daylight so that everyone might see him. The boys went to sleep and after a long time the damp rocket finally shot into the air. He was delighted when he felt himself explode. But nobody saw or heard him. He only frightened a goose who thought it was raining sticks. "I knew I should create a great sensation" ("The Remarkable Rocket," p. 318), gasped the rocket, and he went out.

"The Remarkable Rocket" is one of Wilde's brighter creations. On the surface there seems little to say about it if we resist the temptation to read it as an outgrowth of the controversy between Wilde and James McNeill Whistler. When Wilde reviewed the Grosvenor Gallery Exhibition for the *Dublin University Magazine* in July of 1877, he commented upon Whistler's two *Nocturnes* which showed rockets bursting: "These pictures are certainly worth looking at for about as long as one looks at a real rocket, that is, for somewhat less than a quarter of a minute."[13] No evidence exists to set the exact date of the composition of this story, but we know that Wilde told and retold these stories with many variations before they were ever set down. We know further that the quarrel between Whistler and Wilde reached one of its peaks of intensity in 1888, the year *The Happy Prince and Other Stories* was published. It would have delighted Oscar to have written, with Whistler in mind, the final words of the rocket whose explosion went unnoticed except by a goose.

III   A House of Pomegranates

A House of Pomegranates, published in November of 1891, was dedicated to Constance, Wilde's wife, with individual stories dedicated to other women of his acquaintance. Of the four stories—"The Young King," "The Birthday of the Infanta," "The Fisherman and His Soul," and "The Star-Child"—the first two had been published earlier. This third and last volume, from the stories themselves to the book design, appears to be a much more consciously artistic effort than the others. Walter Crane had designed essentially realistic illustrations for *The Happy Prince and Other Stories*. Charles Ricketts' title page illustration for *A House of Pomegranates*, on the other hand, offers the reader a Pre-Raphaelite maiden somewhat remote from the world of time and reality. In general, as Michael Brooks maintains, "Where Crane imitates Wilde's story, Ricketts creates a visual counterpart to his style."[14]

The viewers were a bit distressed by those very qualities which to Wilde were evidence of the book's artistic distinction. For example, the *Pall Mall Gazette* questioned whether the "Ultra-aestheticism" of the stories made it suitable for children: "The stories are somewhat after the manner of Hans Andersen—and have pretty poetic and imaginative flights like his; but then again they wander off too often into something between a 'Sinburnian ecstasy and the catalogue of a high art furniture dealer.' "[15] The influential *Saturday Review* termed the illustrations "rare and strange in the latest and straitest school of Neo-Preraphaelitism"[16] but found them and the stories pleasing. The comments of the reviewer for *The Speaker* drew a substantial response from Wilde. This reviewer had disliked the cover: "The Indian club with a house-painter's brush on the top which passes muster for a peacock, and the chimney-pot hat with a sponge in it, which is meant to represent a basket containing a pomegranate . . . are grotesque."[17] Wilde, who was very pleased with the design of his book, rose to its defense:

> What the gilt notes suggest, what imitative parallel may be found to them in that chaos that is termed nature, is a matter of no importance. They may suggest, as they do sometimes to me, peacocks and pomegranates and splashing fountains of gold water, or as they do to your critic, sponges and Indian clubs and chimney-pot hats. Such suggestions and evocations have nothing whatsoever to do with the aesthetic quality and value of the design. A thing in Nature becomes much lovelier if it reminds us of a thing in art, but a thing in Art gains no real beauty through reminding us of a thing in Nature. The primary aesthetic impression of a work of art borrows nothing from recognition or resemblance. (*Letters*, p. 301)

Wilde's defense of its design, in perfect correspondence with the principles maintained in *Intentions*, also published in 1891, is an argument based on the primacy of the formal characteristics of art as opposed to those of representationalism. To those like the reviewer for the *Pall Mall Gazette*, who felt the stories were unsuitable for children, Wilde maintained that ". . . in building this *House of Pomegranates* I had about as much intention of pleasing the British child as I had of pleasing the British public" (*Letters*, p. 301).

The first of Wilde's tales concerns a young king who, the night before his coronation, experiences three dreams that reveal to him the deprivation and suffering necessary to maintain him in wealth and luxury. Prior to his mysterious dreams he had been an avid lover of beauty from the moment he had been brought to the palace after the rude existence he had known with the goatherd who had raised him. The young king, so the rumors went, was the son of the king's only daughter who had secretly married an artist working on the cathedral. After his mother and father died under strange circumstances, he was given into the care of the goatherd. His first dream shows him the half-starved women and children who are weaving his coronation robes. He learns that "In war . . . the strong make slaves of the weak, and in peace the rich make slaves of the poor." His second dream reveals the suffering of galley slaves and the terrible death of a diver who brings up a giant pearl for the king's scepter. His third and last dream reveals the dispute between Avarice and Death over the lives of men searching for wealth. Death sends Ague, Fever, and Plague and kills the servants of Avarice toiling for rubies for the king's crown. The next morning when the Chamberlain and other high officers bring him his robe, crown, and scepter, he puts them aside and chooses instead his old leather tunic, sheepskin coat, and shepherd's staff. As he rides to his coronation he is jeered and threatened by his subjects. Even the Bishop in the cathedral, when the young king tells his dreams, advises him to think no more of his dreams. But when the young king kneels before the image of Christ, he is bathed in "a marvellous and mystical light." Then the people and the nobles fall upon their knees and pay him homage while the Bishop cries: "A greater than I hath crowned thee."

"The Young King" provides one of the more striking examples of the outcast figure or stranger in Wilde's stories. Such a figure is found repeatedly in Wilde's work and most notably in such other stories as "The Happy Prince," "The Fisherman and His Soul," and "The Star-Child." The young king is brought from the rough simplicity of the shepherd's life into a world of physical beauty that immediately delights him. But he nevertheless remains an outcast, for it is evident that he is set apart from the other nobles by his finer, more sensitive nature. He worships beauty in solitude.

Wilde also reveals his fascination with the figure of Christ. Wilde's young king is raised in humble circumstances and is about to be made king, but he rejects the raiment and jeweled crown and substitutes instead a shepherd's coat and a circlet of wild briar. He is mocked by the rabble, threatened with death by the nobles, and admonished by the bishop, but as he turns from his prayer at the image of Christ, ". . . lo! through the painted windows came the sunlight streaming upon him, and the sunbeams wove round him a tissued robe that was fairer than the robe that had been fashioned for his pleasure. The dead staff blossomed, and bare lilies that were whiter than pearls. The dry thorn blossomed, and bare roses that were redder than rubies. Whiter than fine pearls were the lilies, and their stems were of bright silver, Redder than male rubies were the roses, and their leaves were of beaten gold" ("The Young King," p. 233). The Christian parallels are obvious. In fact, G. Wilson Knight argues that just as such rich metals are often correlative to transcendence in Biblical literature, in Wilde's story "the flowering metals point a merging of nature into the transcendent,"[18] for at this point the king becomes illuminated by "a marvellous and mystical light" and all did homage.

The elaborate descriptions and catalogues are present in this tale as they are in many of the others, but the manner in which Wilde integrates such descriptions and cataloguings into the overall plan of his story is striking. Wilde had always striven to create an atmosphere of strange and exotic beauty, but he integrates his rich details best in "The Young King."

The second story in Wilde's volume is about the birthday party of the Infanta of Spain. Everything had been done to make this a beautiful and special occasion. On this one day she was allowed to play with other children. Games, mock bullfights, and unusual entertainments had been arranged. Watching it all was the sad king who had never stopped mourning for his queen who had died six months after the birth of their daughter. The dancing of a little dwarf who had been caught running wild in the forest provided the most hilarious part of the morning's entertainment. This little dwarf was delighted by the children's laughter and was particularly struck by the beautiful little Infanta. He was ecstatic when in jest the Infanta threw him her white rose and he learned that she had asked that he dance for her a second time. The dwarf wandered in excitement and happiness into the Infanta's garden, but the tulips, geraniums, lilies, and cactuses were offended by his ugliness. Only the birds liked him for he had given them crumbs in the wintertime. The little dwarf wandered through the many beautiful rooms in the palace until at last he saw a little figure watching him. It was a monster, the most grotesque monster he had ever seen. When he kissed the white rose the little Infanta had given him, the monster did the same. When he realized the truth, he fell to the ground sobbing for there had been no mirror in the forest to show him how he looked. He tore the white rose to bits and lay moaning. At that moment the Infanta and her friends came in and laughed at what they thought was his still funnier acting. When the Infanta commanded him to dance he did not move, for his heart was broken. The Infanta frowned and said disdainfully "For the future let those who come to play with me have no hearts."

Wilde, writing to Robert Ross in 1889, expressed his pleasure at his praise: "I am charmed with what you say about the little Princess—the Infanta in style (in *mere* style as honest Besant would say) it is my best story," (*Letters*, p. 248). Wilde's estimation of his story is sound, for his touch is as certain here as it was in "The Young King." The narrative moves surely with none of the self-conscious moralizing or humor that occasionally mars the tales in his first two volumes. Further, the absence of extraneous descriptive embellishments reveals Wilde's developing skill. The initial description of the Infanta's garden, though strikingly sensuous and ornate, foreshadows the sad ending of the tale: "The purple butterflies fluttered about with gold dust on their wings, visiting each flower in turn; the little lizards crept out of the crevices of the wall, and lay basking in the white glare; and the pomegranates split and cracked with the heat, and showed their bleeding red hearts" ("The Birthday of the Infanta," p. 234).

Wilde creates an effect in the story, partly by the use of his characteristic ornate descriptions, of two levels of reality. One level consists of the Infanta's surface world of elegance, beauty, and laughter and the second consists of an underlying world of sorrow, cruelty, and death. The flowers are beautiful yet cruel to the little dwarf. The Egyptian troop is terrified at the sight of the cruel Don Pedro, but soothed by the beautiful Infanta for "they felt sure that one so lovely as she was could never be cruel to anybody" ("The Birthday of the Infanta," p. 238). Overlooking all the laughter is the sorrowing king whose dead wife, it was suspected, had been killed by Don Pedro. Most poignant is the dwarf's false perception of the beauty and laughter of the children and especially the Infanta. When he is undeceived and perceives both their ugliness and his own, his heart breaks. With great skill, Wilde employs image after image to reinforce the reader's consciousness of the often ironic contrast between these two levels. Wilde is most subtle in this story, and was undoubtedly correct when he insisted that he was not writing for the British child.

"The Fisherman and His Soul," Wilde's third story, is the longest of the tales in *A House of Pomegranates*. In fact, it is nearly as long as the entire *Happy Prince* collection. Unlike "Lord Arthur Savile's Crime," which equals it in length, the narrative is rambling and somewhat tedious. A good portion of the narrative problem stems from Wilde's mismanagement of point of view. The narrative focuses initially upon the fisherman, but Wilde lavishes most of his attention upon the fisherman's soul. The soul travels far and has many adventures when separated from the fisherman and is given almost all the opportunities to tell about them in the usual ornate Wildean prose. Furthermore, the central conflict of the story is divided between the efforts of the fisherman to live with his mermaid in the sea and the struggle of the soul to be reunited with his body. Not only is the central conflict uncertain, but the fisherman's soul commands most of the reader's interest. The ending lends equal if not greater ambiguity to the meaning of the story. To keep his love the fisherman must give up his soul, yet the loss of his soul is presented as an unacceptable alternative.

"The Star-Child," the last story in A *House of Pomegranates*, represents another variation of the story of the outcast or stranger with its attendant themes of pain, suffering, and love. Powerfully present also is Wilde's deep concern with social issues, especially the inequities in the distribution of the good things of life and the hardening of hearts that poverty and hardship bring. Although the Star-Child is described in conventional Wildean terms, ". . . he was white and delicate as sown ivory, and his curls were like the rings of the daffodil" ("The Star-Child," p. 276), "The Star-Child" is without much of the usual adjectival embroidery found in such tales as "The Young King" or "The Fisherman and His Soul." This is also the only tale in which beauty, in this case the Star-Child's personal beauty, serves as the direct source of pride, cruelty, and selfishness. Like the conclusions of "The Young King," "The Selfish Giant," and "The Happy Prince" the outcast achieves transcendence through love. Nevertheless, Wilde's concluding line encourages speculation concerning the possible weakening of Wilde's certainty about the capacity of love to create an enduring good.

CHAPTER 4

Criticism

O SCAR Wilde loved to shock people with clever inversions and
startling paradoxes. When affronting Philistine conventional-
ity he might assert that "An ethical sympathy in an artist is an
unpardonable mannerism of style ("Preface," *The Picture of Dorian
Gray*). When attacking the mimetic or other approaches to art he
might insist that "the only real people are those who never existed"
("Decay of Lying," p. 297) or, even more startling coming as it does
from a supposed romantic, that "All bad poetry springs from
genuine feeling" ("Critic as Artist, II," p. 398). As a consequence of
these and other "excesses," Wilde's criticism has often been termed
superficial, inconsistent, contradictory, and even insincere. Graham
Hough argues in *The Last Romantics* that "Wildean aestheticism
was little more than a series of attitudes and undigested notions,
held together for the time by what must once have been a brilliant
and attractive personality."[1] Jerome Buckley in *The Victorian Temper* informs us that Wilde and his ilk "suffered—or affected to
suffer—the ineffable weariness of strayed revelers lost in a palace of
fading illusion."[2] Others, such as René Wellek, classify Wilde as a
"new romantic."[3] But to dismiss Wilde and his criticism as only a
manifestation of the end of an exhausted century or a reworking in
decadent[4] terms of an older romanticism is to see Wilde's work
incompletely. Wilde, as Richard Ellmann suggests, "Laid the basis
for many critical positions which are still debated in much the same
terms and which we like to attribute to more ponderous names."[5]

The links between Oscar Wilde's critical ideas and those of such
Romantics as Samuel Taylor Coleridge, John Keats, Percy Bysshe
Shelly, Lord Byron, Johann Wolfgang von Goethe, Friedrich Schil-
ler, and Thomas Carlyle, along with the many figures associated
with the Pre-Raphaelite Movement were certainly important. But
Wilde's critical ties to his own era are, of course, central. The role of

73

criticism, for example, as a means of enriching life was an idea
derived from Matthew Arnold. Although Arnold argued in "The
Function of Criticism" that the critical power is of lower rank than
the creative, he also observed that this supremacy cannot be maintained in all epochs. Criticism sometimes can only prepare the
ground for later creative resurgences. A study of Wilde's major
critical writing, especially "The Critic as Artist," indicates that
Wilde shared Arnold's understanding of the historical changes in the
critic's role. Arnold's concern with organic form in art as expressed
in his "Preface to the Poems of 1853" is also shared by Wilde. On
the other hand, their critical views diverged in significant ways.
Arnold, for example, argued that "It is the business of the critical
power . . . to see the object as in itself it really is" ("The Function of
Criticism at the Present Time"). Wilde insists in "The Critic as
Artist" that "the primary aim of the critic is to see the object as in
itself it really is not" ("Critic as Artist, I," p. 369). Such subjectivity
was unacceptable to Arnold, a critic very much a part of his age in
his desire for objectivity and certitude.

The ideas of John Ruskin and William Morris also had a powerful
shaping influence upon Wilde's thought. In both men we find a
strong concern for social justice, a belief in individual labor and
handicraft activity, a rejection of modern civilization in favor of a
romanticized medieval one, and a belief that the pursuit of beauty or
an imaginative world of perfection of being can be the only valid
quest amidst the hideous realities of modern industrial England.
The influence of these two men is most apparent in "The Soul of
Man Under Socialism," his writings on the decorative arts, "The
English Renaissance of Art," "De Profundis," and *Intentions*.
Wilde's romanticism fuses under the influence of these two men
into what San Juan Epifanio, Jr. terms "a curious form of artistic
individualism he calls 'socialism.' "[6] It also creates an inevitable
conflict between an ideal of art that is rooted in craftsmanship and
designed to serve the moral good of a people and an art that exists as
pure form, an end in itself, whose purpose is individual delight.

Walter Pater, a critic who presented a philosophy of art and life
much closer than Arnold, Ruskin, or Morris' to the twentieth century, exerted the most immediate and profound influence upon
Oscar Wilde. Pater's radical skepticism accepted the universe as
mechanism. From this skepticism followed the belief that examining
one's private experience is a more fruitful pursuit than thinking

about the external universe. The aim of life became the deepest response to what is beautiful, curious, or profound. The artist's role, consequently, is not to teach lessons or stimulate us to good, but to reveal to us the most striking impressions of which his nature is capable. Thus, the art which he creates should strive "to be independent of the mere intelligence, to become a matter of pure perception, to get rid of its responsibilities to its subject or material" ("School of Giorgione," *The Renaissance*). Pater's "Art for Art's Sake" position was a far cry from the Arnoldian critical stance. Pater's view of the role of the critic conflicts in a fundamental way with Arnold's dictum that he must see the object as it really is. Pater argues in his "Preface" to *The Renaissance* that "in aesthetic criticism the first step toward seeing one's object as it really is, is to know one's own impression as it really is, to discriminate it, to realize it distinctly."

I   Intentions

In *Intentions*, the collection of essays that Wilde published in 1891, we find the basic expressions of Wilde's critical thought. Although other essays such as "The Rise of Historical Criticism" (1877), "The Soul of Man Under Socialism" (1891), and "De Profundis" (1906, 1960) contain elements of Wilde's critical thinking, *Intentions* presents them in his most attractive style. On the surface the essays are written in a style that appears insouciant, extravagant, and paradoxical; but beneath that surface lay Wilde's central critical beliefs concerning the relationships of life and art, ideas which informed not only his written works but his life. Wilde was delighted with his work as he indicated four years later to Ada Leverson: "I simply love that book" (*Letters*, p. 373). Wilde's critical audience responded to *Intentions* with praise for the freshness, originality, and brilliance of his ideas and wit and with a considerable degree of exasperation with his verbal excesses and intellectual affectation. But there was surprisingly little serious discussion of Wilde's ideas.

II   *"The Decay of Lying"*

"The Decay of Lying," the first essay in *Intentions*, first appeared in *Nineteenth Century* in January of 1889.[7] The issues of "The Decay of Lying," as in most of Wilde's critical writings, center around the fundamental problem of the relationship of life to art. Its structure takes the form of a dialogue between two friends, Cyril and Vivian.[8]

Vivian, who does most of the talking in the dialogue, sets forth the views of Wilde. Cyril, on the other hand, expresses more conventional critical attitudes. Because the basic issues in *Intentions* concern the relationship between Art and Nature, it is appropriate that Wilde's "Decay of Lying" should begin with Cyril, the conventional interlocutor, entering the library of a country house in Nottinghamshire through an open window. It is a lovely afternoon and Cyril, who like William Wordsworth's speaker in "The Tables Turned" believes in "one impulse from a vernal wood," urges him to come out, lie on the grass, and enjoy Nature. Vivian replies that he has lost the capacity to enjoy Nature for his study of Art has revealed "Nature's lack of design, her curious crudities, her extraordinary monotony, her absolute unfinished condition" ("Decay of Lying," pp. 290-291). Although Nature has good intentions "she cannot carry them out" and as for enjoying Nature: ". . . Nature is so uncomfortable. Grass is hard and lumpy and damp, and full of dreadful black insects. Why, even Morris' poorest workman could make you a more comfortable seat than the whole of Nature can. . . . If Nature had been comfortable, mankind would never have invented architecture, and I prefer houses to the open air" ("Decay of Lying," p. 291). Vivian, speaking for Wilde, rejects the conventional view of Nature as a beneficient universe with which man seeks to exist harmoniously. He sees it rather as an incomplete extrinsic environment which must be shaped to accommodate man. Thus, Vivian rejects Cyril's invitation in order to remain indoors to put the finishing touches upon the proofs of his article "The Decay of Lying."

Vivian reveals that the most serious evidence of the decay of lying can be seen in the work of the modern novelist who "presents us with dull facts under the guise of fiction" ("Decay of Lying," p. 293). He has not even the "courage of other people's ideas; but insists on going directly to life for everything" ("The Decay of Lying," p. 293). Such practices are fatal to the creative imagination. The danger is that Robert Louis Stevenson's *Dr. Jekyl and Mr. Hyde* reads dangerously like an experiment out of the *Lancet* and Mr. Henry James "writes fiction as if it were a painful duty." Wilde's point, of course, is that art, in this case fiction, consists of the shaping of the raw materials of Nature by the artist's mind into an artificial form which hitherto existed nowhere in Nature. Hence, any attempt at going directly to Nature, as an Emile Zola would urge, can lead only to bad art. Only through the conscious work of the artist can a sense of reality be achieved. Hence, the essential truth of Vivian's paradoxical statement that "The only real people are the people who never existed" ("The Decay of Lying," p. 297). The work of art then is autonomous. It "never expresses anything but itself" and exists independent of Nature.

If art finds its own perfection within, and not outside of itself, then art must be judged in terms of itself, in terms of how nearly it realizes the possibility of perfection inherent in its matter. Vivian also suggests that art simultaneously seeks to realize Platonic "ideal" forms as well as to fulfill the terms of the great archetypes: "Hers are the 'forms more real than living man,' and hers the great archetypes of which things that have existence are but unfinished copies. Nature has, in her eyes, no laws, no uniformity" ("The Decay of Lying," p. 306). Vivian follows up the above approximation of Platonic doctrine with the already-quoted paradox that "Life imitates Art far more than Art imitates life." Cyril, of course, seems to accept this curious theory, but argues that to make it complete Vivian must show that "Nature, no less than Life, is an imitation of Art" ("Decay of Lying," p. 311). Vivian, unabashed, proceeds to argue that Nature takes many of its effects from the landscape painter:

Where, if not from the Impressionists, do we get those wonderful brown fogs that come creeping down our streets, blurring the gas-lamps and changing the houses into monstrous shadows? To whom, if not to them and their master, do we owe the lovely silver mists that brood over our river, and turn to faint forms of fading grace curved bridge and swaying barge? The extraordinary change that has taken place in the climate of London during the last ten years is entirely due to this particular school of Art. You smile. Consider the matter from a scientific or metaphysical point of view, and you will find that I am right. For what is Nature? Nature is no great mother who has borne us. She is our creation. It is in our brain that she quickens to life. Things are because we see them, and what we see, and how we see it, depends on the Arts that have influenced us. To look at a thing is very different from seeing a thing. One does not see anything until one sees its beauty. Then, and then only, does it come into existence. At present, people see fogs, not because there are fogs, but because poets and painters have taught them the mysterious loveliness of such effects. There may have been fogs for centuries in London. I dare say there were. But no one saw them, and so we do not know anything about them. They did not exist till Art had invented them. ("The Decay of Lying," p. 312)

From the point of view of our own time the apparently absurd notion that Nature imitates Art is a perfectly sound one. Anthropology and psychology readily acknowledge today that by means of language human beings organize their impressions, memories, and anticipations into highly individual and articulated designs. The raw outer world unless symbolically organized by language, ritual, or more specifically by the forms of art, as Wilde would have it, would be perceived as essentially chaotic.[9]

At the close of the essay Vivian, Wilde's obvious spokesman, summarizes the doctrines of the "new aesthetics":

> Art never expresses anything but itself. It has an independent life, just as Thought has, and develops purely on its own lines . . . . The second doctrine is this. All bad art comes from returning to Life and Nature, and elevating them into ideals. Life and Nature may sometimes be used as part of Art's rough material, but before they are of any real service to art they must be translated into artistic conventions . . . . The third doctrine is that Life imitates Art far more than Art imitates Life. . . . It follows, as a corollary from this, that external Nature also imitates Art. . . . The final revelation is that Lying, the telling of beautiful untrue things, is the proper aim of Art. ("Decay of Lying," pp. 319-320)

"The Decay of Lying" is one of the most enjoyable of Wilde's prose writings. The tone of the essay is playful and light with Cyril's earnest and conventional appreciation of the beauty and perfection of external nature set against Vivian's languid, good-humored undercutting of Cyril's simple Romantic attitudes. Much of Wilde's effect is achieved by alternating brilliant epigrammatic passages with long Impressionistic, even rhapsodic, passages of prose.

The most abundant form of epigram Wilde employs is the paradox created by the inversion of some commonly held truth—for example, in the case of fictional characters, "the only real people are the people who never existed" ("Decay of Lying," p. 297), or in the case of the legal profession, "They can make the worse appear the better cause . . . and have been known to wrest from reluctant juries triumphant verdicts of acquittal for their clients, even when those clients, as often happens, were clearly and unmistakably innocent" ("Decay of Lying," p. 292); and, in the case of Wordsworth, ". . . he was never a lake poet. He found in stones the sermons he had already hidden there" ("Decay of Lying," p. 301). The second kind of epigram consists of a brief, usually facetious, parody of one of society's critical or moralistic clichés. During their discussion of fiction Vivian argues that "the fashion of lying has almost fallen into disrepute" ("The Decay of Lying," p. 294). The consequence is that one tends to develop a "morbid and unhealthy faculty of truth-telling . . . and often ends by writing novels which are so like life that no one can possibly believe in their probability" ("Decay of Lying," p. 294). Thus, Vivian, in epigrammatic form, parodies the conventional cliché that realistic art by the careful reproduction of life achieves verisimilitude.

The other stylistic device Wilde utilizes is the long Impressionistic "purple" passage. The impressionism of such passages is deliberately exaggerated and calculated to amuse us, but within Wilde's Paterian swellings and digressions are implanted Wilde's critical ideas whether stated in the form of paradox or not. In the passage that follows, Vivian complains of critics who judge art by the degree to which it mirrors life:

> No doubt there will always be critics who like a certain writer in the *Saturday Review*, will gravely censure the teller of fairy tales for his defective knowledge of natural history, who will measure imaginative work by their own lack of any imaginative faculty, and will hold up their inkstained hands in horror if some honest gentleman, who has never been farther than the yew-trees of his own garden, pens a fascinating book of travels like Sir John Mandeville, or, like great Raleigh, writes a whole history of the world, without knowing anything whatsoever about the past. To excuse themselves they will try and shelter under the shield of him who made Prospero the magician, and gave him Caliban and Ariel as his servants, who heard the Tritons blowing their horns round the coral reefs of the Enchanted Isle, and the fairies singing to each other in a wood near Athens, who led the phantom kings in dim procession across the misty Scottish heath, and hid Hecate in a cave with the weird sisters. They will call upon Shakespeare—they always do—and will quote that hackneyed passage about Art holding the mirror up to Nature, forgetting that this unfortunate aphorism is deliberately said by Hamlet in order to convince the bystanders of his absolute insanity in all art-matters. ("Decay of Lying," pp. 305-306)

What Wilde cleverly demonstrates is the exact converse of the rule of the critic who judges a work's success on its degree of realism. He reveals in exaggerated prose that what we find in Shakespeare's work is the enchantment of his created literary world rather than his ability to capture the reality of existence.

III   *"Pen, Pencil and Poison"*

The second essay in *Intentions*, "Pen, Pencil and Poison: A Study in Green," first appeared in *The Fortnightly Review* in

January, 1889. This short account of the life of Thomas Griffiths Wainewright (1794–1852) begins with the observation that artists and men of letters have often been the subject of reproach because "they are lacking in wholeness and completeness of nature" ("Pen, Pencil and Poison," p. 320). Wainewright, Wilde points out, although of an extremely artistic temperament, followed many masters: ". . . being not merely a poet and a painter, an art-critic, an antiquarian, and a writer of prose, an amateur of beautiful things, and a dilettante of things delightful, but also a forger of no mean or ordinary capabilities, and as a subtle and secret poisoner almost without rival in this or any age" ("Pen, Pencil and Poison," p. 321).

The tone of Wilde's essay is three-layered in a sense. On the surface it appears serious; but in spite of Wilde's straight-faced praise of Wainewright as a "subtle and secret poisoner without rival" or later his attribution to Wainewright of such a banality as "In art . . . whatever is worth doing at all is worth doing well," the reader quickly recognizes that below this first layer of apparent seriousness lies a tone of amusing and playful banter. Yet, if one reads the essay carefully, it becomes apparent that Wilde means everything he says. He does not, of course, approve murder, but he sets forth most of the fundamental tenets of his artistic credo. The same epigrammatic style that Wilde employs in "The Decay of Lying" is found in this essay only in more subdued form. Paradoxes and inversions of commonly held truths are interwoven with flights of purple Impressionistic prose.

After a brief military career and a period of deep melancholia, Wainewright took up literature as an art. He wrote papers on artistic subjects, usually under fanciful pseudonyms, and assumed "grotesque masks" under which to "hide his seriousness, or to reveal his levity . . . . A mask tells us more than a face. These disguises intensified his personality" ("Pen, Pencil and Poison," p. 323). Significantly, Wilde is describing his own method as well as his own dandyism when he tells us how Wainewright "determined to startle the town as a dandy, and his beautiful rings, his antique cameo breast-pin, and his pale lemon-coloured kid gloves, were wellknown . . ." ("Pen, Pencil and Poison," p. 323). Wilde facetiously admits that if we set aside his achievements with strychnine what is left hardly justifies his reputation: "But then it is only the Philistine who seeks to estimate a personality by the vulgar test of production. This young dandy sought to be somebody, rather than to do something. He recognized that Life itself is an art, and has its modes of style no less than the arts that seek to express it" ("Pen, Pencil and Poison," p. 324).

Such expressions of Wilde's theories of personality remind us of *The Picture of Dorian Gray,* written in 1890 a year after "Pen, Pencil and Poison," and Lord Henry Wotton's dicta concerning personality. Clearly Wilde has a Dorian Gray-like life and personality in mind, for immediately following the above description of Wainewright's dandyism are long passages describing his sensitivity to beautiful surroundings, interior decoration, exotic statuary, beautifully bound books, engravings, and so forth that immediately remind the reader of the eleventh chapter of *The Picture of Dorian Gray.*

Wainewright's greatest distinction came from his artistry as a poisoner. But Wilde appears not so much interested in his cleverness with strychnine as he is in the effects of sin upon the personality. In "The Critic as Artist" Wilde had argued that "Sin increases the experience of the race. Through its intensified assertion of individualism, it saves us from monotony of type" ("Critic as Artist," p. 360). In "Pen, Pencil and Poison" Wilde argues that Wainewright's crimes had an important effect upon his art: "They gave a strong personality to his style, a quality that his early work certainly lacked" ("Pen, Pencil and Poison," p. 338). Wilde is, by no means, condoning murder. He means by the above statement that crime because it is an unusual, rare, and forceful event in any person's life will probably produce in a given personality unusual, rare, and powerful effects. These effects, of course, are grist for any artist's mill. To question the morality of the act is beside the question: "The fact of a man being a poisoner is nothing against his prose" ("Pen, Pencil and Poison," p. 339). Wilde does, however, deliberately and humorously confuse the issue for he maintains that when Wainewright was reproached for the murder of Helen Abercrombie, he shrugged his shoulders and said, "Yes, it was a dreadful thing to do, but she had very thick ankles" ("Pen, Pencil and Poison," p. 337).

IV   *"Critic as Artist"*

The "Critic as Artist" was published in two parts. The first part, "The Critic as Artist: With Some Remarks Upon the Importance of Doing Nothing," was published in *Nineteenth Century* in July, 1890, while the second part, "The Critic as Artist: With Some Remarks

Upon the Importance of Discussing Everything," appeared in September, 1890. Both essays, like "The Decay of Lying," are in dialogue form. The overall concern, the relationship between art and life, is the same as in Wilde's "The Decay of Lying." The dialogue, in this case between Ernest, the straightforward interlocutor, and Gilbert, the subtle spokesman for Wilde's credo, duplicates in style and tone the dialogue between Cyril and Vivian with its blend of epigram and long Impressionistic passages.

The dialogue in "The Critic as Artist: With Some Remarks Upon the Importance of Doing Nothing" takes place in the library of a house in Piccadilly overlooking Green Park. Ernest interrupts Gilbert's piano-playing with the observation that most volumes of reminiscences are banal and become interesting only when authors write about themselves, not others. This leads to a discussion of criticism, especially art criticism, a pursuit which Ernest feels is unjustified: "Why cannot the artist be left alone, to create a new world if he wishes it, or, if not, to shadow forth the world which we already know, and of which, I fancy, we would each one of us be wearied if Art, with her fine spirit of choice and delicate instinct of selection, did not, as it were, purify it for us, and give it a momentary perfection. . . . Why should those who cannot create take upon themselves to estimate the value of creative work?" ("Critic as Artist," I, p. 344) Ernest then asserts "that in the best days of art there were no art critics" ("Critic as Artist," I, p. 346) and follows with a long Impressionistic account of the creative arts of Greece. Gilbert praises Ernest for his "terribly unsound" but "delightfully unreal" account of the relation of the Hellenic artist to the intellectual spirit of his age, but insists that the Greeks were a "nation of art-critics" and that our primary debt to the Greeks was for the "critical spirit" ("Critic as Artist," I, p. 350). This "critical spirit" was exercised on the two highest arts, according to Gilbert, "Life and Literature." This critical spirit was concerned not with the moral but the purely aesthetic criticism of art. Hence, the critic is concerned like Aristotle and Goethe primarily with the impression a work produces ("Critic as Artist," I, p. 353).

Ernest insists, notwithstanding, that the creative faculty is higher than the critical. Gilbert replies that "Without the critical faculty, there is no artistic creation at all, worthy of the name" ("Critic as Artist," I, p. 355). At this point, Gilbert mentions Arnold's famous definition of literature as a criticism of life as evidence, if "not very

felicitous in form," of "how keenly he recognized the importance of
the critical element in all creative work." Gilbert further maintains
that because all great art is "self-conscious and deliberate," there
has never been a creative age that has not been critical also: "For it
is the critical faculty that invents fresh forms. The tendency of creation is to repeat itself. It is to the critical instinct that we owe each
new school that springs up, each new world that art finds ready to its
hand" ("Critic as Artist," I, p. 357). Gilbert concludes his argument
on the relationship of the artist and the critic by insisting that "criticism demands infinitely more cultivation than creation does"
("Critic as Artist," I, p. 358) and that it is "very much more difficult
to talk about a thing than to do it" ("Critic as Artist," I, p. 359).

The second issue in the essay, the relationship of the artist to life,
is touched upon when Gilbert in connection with his arguments
about the superiority of criticism to creation argues that "Anybody
can make history. Only a great man can write it." After a beautiful
Impressionistic passage extolling the perfection of an art eternal in
its beauty in contrast to the mere instants of life that most of us
know, Ernest sums up Gilbert's, or Wilde's, notions of the relationship of art to life:

It may, indeed, be that life is chaos, as you tell me that it is; that its
martyrdoms are mean and its heroisms ignoble; and that it is the function of
Literature to create, from the rough material of actual existence, a new
world that will be more marvelous, more enduring, and more true than the
world that common eyes look upon, and through which common natures
seek to realize their perfection. But surely, if this new world has been made
by the spirit and touch of a great artist, it will be a thing so complete and
perfect that there will be nothing left for the critic to do. ("Critic as Artist,"
I, pp. 363-364)

Gilbert replies that "The critic occupies the same relation to the
work of art that he criticizes as the artist does to the visible world of
form and colour, or the unseen world of passion and of thought"
("Critic as Artist," I, p. 364). Thus, the critic's work is a "creation
within a creation." The best criticism because it is "the purest form
of personal impression, is in its way more creative than creation, as
it has least reference to any standard external to itself, and is, in fact,
its own reason for existing . . ." ("Critic as Artist," I, p. 365). Gilbert argues for a criticism that is Impressionistic and autonomous.
However, the autonomy is not that of the work but that of the artist.

The "work of art is simply the starting-point for a new creation" ("Critic as Artist," I, p. 367). The primary emphasis is upon the impressions of the critic. The accuracy or wholeness with which he perceives either life or the art form are unimportant. Life and art are only raw materials out of which the critic, the higher artist, fashions beauty. Gilbert maintains that Arnold's famous statement from "On the Function of Criticism at the Present Time" (1864) that "the proper aim of criticism is to see the object as in itself it really is" ("Critic as Artist," I, p. 366), is a very serious error. Nor does Gilbert or Wilde accept Walter Pater's view in Studies in the History of the Renaissance (1873) that "the first step towards seeing one's object as it really is, is to know one's own impression as it really is, to discriminate it, to realize it distinctly." Gilbert argues that "the primary aim of the critic is to see the object as in itself it really is not" ("Critic as Artist," I, p. 369). He means by this that the critic uses his impressions of a work as a stepping-stone towards a personal perception of beauty that exceeds the original work of art.

The second part of "The Artist as Critic" provides further developments of the issues of part one but emphasizes the relationships of the critic to life and society and the qualities and function of the critic. Gilbert, in part one, had concluded that music was the perfect type of art because "Music can never reveal its ultimate secret" and thus enables the Impressionistic critic to achieve the highest creativity. But in part two he argues that the Impressionist can succeed in interpreting the work and personality of others only to the degree that he succeeds in intensifying his own personality, for "the more strongly this personality enters into the interpretation the more real the interpretation becomes, the more satisfying, the more convincing, and the more true" ("Critic as Artist," II, p. 373). Gilbert feels that because the critic's impressions of an art work are shaped by the nature of personality, the critic must make the cultivation of his own his lifelong work. He becomes, as it were, a work of art. This idea forms the basis of Oscar Wilde's theory of personality so well fictionalized in The Picture of Dorian Gray.

Although Wilde generally insists upon artistic and critical individualism throughout Intentions, in the "Critic as Artist" he presents another idea that is distinctly non-individualistic. Although the artist must intensify his own individualism, when he does so successfully he gains access to a spiritual entity that is racial or collective, not individual. Wilde maintains that "just as Nature is matter struggling into mind, so Art is mind expressing itself under the conditions of matter, and thus, even in the lowliest of her manifestations, she speaks to both sense and soul alike." Wilde and Carlyle may at first glance seem strange bedfellows but a glance at *Sartor Resartus* and *On Heroes, Hero-Worship and the Heroic in History* confirms the existence in both of a Romantic idealism but, in Wilde's case, a non-transcendental idealism stripped of its Puritan trappings. Wilde built his critical views upon certain Romantic ways of looking at the relationship between the individual and Nature or objective reality, but to Wilde any meanings inherent in the forms which man produces out of the chaos of the world begin and end in himself. No Carlylean Oversoul exists behind the mask of Nature for Wilde. Thus, when Wilde in "The Critic as Artist" speaks of the soul within us as something more than a single spiritual entity, his words are best understood as a striking anticipation of Jungian archetypes rather than a form of Romantic idealism. For to Wilde, "By revealing to us the absolute mechanism of all action, and so freeing us from the self-imposed and trammeling burden of moral responsibility, the scientific principle of Heredity has become, as it were, the warrant for the contemplative life" ("Critic as Artist," II, pp. 382-383). This contemplative life leads us into contact with an imaginative life greater than that of any individual: ". . . it is not our own life that we live, but the lives of the dead, and the soul that dwells within us is no single spiritual entity, making us personal and individual, created for our service, and entering into us for our joy. It is something that has dwelt in fearful places, and in ancient sepulchres has made its abodes. It is sick with many maladies, and has memories of curious sins. It is wiser than we are, and its wisdom is bitter" ("Critic as Artist," II, p. 383). Wilde calls this capacity for extending ourselves the imagination: "Yes, it is the imagination; and the imagination is the result of heredity. It is simply concentrated race-experience" ("Critic as Artist," II, p. 384). This is not the Romantic imagination of Keats' "viewless wings of poesy" but an incomplete rendering of racial archetypes.

The critic then has a social function in that his access to such racial experiences helps him transmit these to the culture. This is the source of whatever utility the critical spirit possesses. One by-product of this transmission is that a nation becomes cosmopolitan.

By the cultivation of intellectual criticism a nation will rise superior to racial prejudices and this may be a starting-point, according to Gilbert, for the elimination of war.

What are the qualities of the critic and how is he to function in the world? In response to Ernest's question Gilbert sets forth another idea that is startling in its contemporaneity. The function of contemplative life "has for its aim not *doing* but *being*, and not *being* merely, but *becoming*—that is what the critical spirit can give us" ("Critic as Artist," II, p. 384). The similarity to twentieth century Existential thought is evident. Wilde fictionalizes this process in his novel with Dorian Gray and Lord Henry Wotton representing artist-critics involved in this Existential process with mixed success. Lord Henry succeeds where Dorian fails because in performing his artistic-critical function Wilde's artist rejects Nature as the ideal of beauty, for the real artist proceeds "not from feeling to form, but from form to thought and passion" ("Critic as Artist," II, p. 398). The true artist is detached from life: "It is just because he has no new message, that he can do beautiful work. He gains his inspiration from form, and from form purely, as an artist should. A real passion would ruin him. Whatever actually occurs is spoiled for art. All bad poetry springs from genuine feeling. To be natural is to be obvious, and to be obvious is to be inartistic" ("Critic as Artist," II, p. 398). The artist or critic, like Lord Henry, is the detached observer of life. His total concern with form enables him to achieve this objectivity. Because true art does not incite men to action, it is outside of the sphere of ethics. Hence, all art is "immoral."

Wilde is careful to make a distinction, however, between the function of the true critic and that of the true artist. Gilbert insists that "a really great artist can never judge of other people's work at all, and can hardly, in fact, judge of his own. That very concentration of vision that makes a man an artist, limits by its sheer intensity ·his faculty of fine appreciation" ("Critic as Artist," II, p. 400). It is only the aesthetic critic who creates nothing himself who can judge art, for technique, according to Wilde, is personality and cannot be learned or taught: "It is exactly because a man cannot do a thing that he is the proper judge of it" ("Critic as Artist," II, p. 401). Thus, "The aesthetic critic, and the aesthetic critic alone, can appreciate all forms and modes. It is to him that Art makes her appeal" ("Critic as Artist," II, p. 401).

Near the close of "The Critic as Artist" Gilbert, in heightened terms, explains the parallel of aesthetics to Darwinian natural selection and, once again, reveals a degree of social purpose beneath his aesthetics:

Aesthetics, in fact, are to Ethics in the sphere of conscious civilization, what, in the sphere of the external world, sexual is to natural selection. Ethics, like natural selection, makes existence possible. Aesthetics, like sexual selection, make life lovely and wonderful, fill it with new forms, and give it progress, and variety and change. And when we reach the true culture that is our aim, we attain to that perfection of which the saints have dreamed, the perfection of those to whom sin is impossible, not because they make the renunciations of the ascetic, but because they can do everything they wish without hurt to the soul, and can wish for nothing that can do the soul harm, the soul being an entity so divine that it is able to transform into elements of a richer experience, or a finer susceptibility, or a newer mode of thought, acts or passions that with the common would be commonplace, or with the uneducated ignoble, or with the shameful vile. Is this dangerous? Yes; it is dangerous—all ideas, as I told you, are so. ("Critic as Artist," II, pp. 406-407)

Thus, Wilde sets forth a theory of aesthetic progress in "The Critic as Artist" that suggests that even Oscar Wilde possessed his share of Victorian earnestness. His theories are hardly complete or consistent but their outlines are clear. Wilde was not a careful, systematic thinker nor did he attempt to be. To suggest or to communicate an impression was enough. He was like Gilbert in "The Critic as Artist," who at the end of the essay admits that he is a dreamer: "Yes, I am a dreamer. For a dreamer is one who can only find his way by moonlight, and his punishment is that he sees the dawn before the rest of the world" ("Critic as Artist," II, p. 407).

V   *"The Truth of Masks"*

The "Truth of Masks: A Note on Illusion," the fourth and last essay in Oscar Wilde's *Intentions*, first appeared under the title "Shakespeare and Stage Costume" in May 1885 in *Nineteenth Century*. This is probably the weakest of the essays in *Intentions*. Wilde's thesis is perfectly sound, but Wilde is not at his stylistic best. Absent are the brilliant epigrams and prose flights of the other essays. Nonetheless, "The Truth of Masks" is well organized and richly imbued with fascinating details of Shakespeare's concern with costume. The essay also helps shed additional light on Wilde's ideas concerning the relationship between realism and realistic detail in art.

Wilde uses as the occasion of his essay an article in *Nineteenth Century* by Lord Lytton setting forth the view that any concern for fidelity of costume in the staging of Shakespeare's plays is inappropriate and pointless.[10] Wilde responds by emphasizing that Shakespeare introduced masques and dances not only for visual pleasure but for their importance as a means of producing certain dramatic effects. For example, "Many of his plays . . . depend for their illusion on the character of the various dresses worn by the hero or the heroine . . ." ("Truth of Masks," p. 409). Wilde points out the "almost numberless" occasions when Shakespeare makes use of disguises and employs costume that utilizes even small details of dress as a means of intensifying dramatic situations. Shakespeare's metaphors are frequently drawn from dress; and, according to Wilde, "It may be worth while to remind people that the whole of the Philosophy of Clothes is to be found in Lear's scene with Edgar—a passage which has the advantage of brevity and style over the grotesque wisdom and somewhat mouthing metaphysics of *Sartor Resartus*" ("Truth of Masks," p. 415).

The latter portions of "The Truth of Masks" contain more emphasis upon Wilde's artistic ideas. The essential autonomy of art is stressed: ". . . it should be remembered that Art has no other aim but her own perfection, and proceeds simply by her own laws" ("Truth of Masks," p. 426). However, the emphasis upon beauty that is so strong in "The Decay of Lying" or "The Critic as Artist" is diminished. Beauty in "The Truth of Masks" seems a desirable accompaniment of the highest art but not the chief end: ". . . neither in costume nor in dialogue is beauty the dramatist's primary aim at all. The true dramatist aims first at what is characteristic, and no more desires that all his personages should be beautifully attired than he desires that they should all have beautiful natures or speak beautiful English. The true dramatist, in fact, shows us life under the conditions of art, not art in the form of life" ("Truth of Masks," p. 428). If we recall that this essay first appeared in 1885 or four to five years earlier than the other essays in *Intentions*, we should not be surprised that these early ideas do not harmonize with the critical principles of the later essays. Wilde would not have said in 1890 that

art "shows us life under the conditions of art." Although this repre-
sents no real contradiction of the critical principles of "The Critic as
Artist," the emphasis in the later essays is upon the remoteness of
Art from real life and the primacy of the beauty of form.

VI *"The Portrait of Mr. W. H."*

Oscar Wilde's other piece of Shakespearean criticism, "The Portrait of Mr. W. H.," first appeared in *Blackwood's Edinburgh
Magazine* in July 1889, four years after "The Truth of Masks."[11] It
stemmed from Wilde's own fascination with the Willie Hughes
theory and his idea that when a person convinces another of some
idea, he inevitably loses his own belief. The idea in question is the
belief of Wilde's character, Cyril Graham, that the dedication to the
1609 edition of Shakespeare's sonnets is intended for a boy-actor in
Shakespeare's theatre, a Mr. Will Hughes.[12] The actual dedication
is as follows: "To the Onlie Begetter Of These Insuing Sonnets, Mr.
W. H. All Happiness And That Eternitie Promised by Our Ever-
Living Poet Wisheth Thee Well-Wishing Adventurer in Setting
Forth, T. T." Wilde's critical work in this instance, unlike the four
pieces in *Intentions*, is put into fictional form.

Wilde's narrator, during a discussion of literary forgeries, is
shown by his friend Erskine a small full-length portrait of a young
man in sixteenth century costume. Erskine explains to the puzzled
narrator that this is the portrait of Mr. W. H., "the Onlie Begetter"
of Shakespeare's sonnets.[13] Erskine then tells the story of Cyril
Graham's theory that the "Mr. W. H." mentioned in the dedication
was a boy-actor in Shakespeare's company. Unable to find historical
proof of the existence of Willie Hughes, Cyril Graham had the
portrait painted as final proof of the boy's existence.[14] Erskine,
however, discovered the forgery and reproached Graham for his
deception. After bequeathing the portrait to Erskine, Graham shot
himself. The narrator after hearing Erskine's account becomes concerned about the truth of Graham's theory and sets to work to prove
it. Having convinced himself of the soundness of the theory, he
writes a letter setting forth his ideas to Erskine. No sooner has he
finished the letter, however, than his faith in the theory evaporates.
But Erskine, now convinced of its truth, goes to Germany to continue the research. Two years later he writes to the narrator explaining that he has failed to find any new evidence and has determined
to take his life as Graham had in order to convince him of its truth.

The narrator, horrified, rushes to Europe only to find that his friend did not take his life but before dying of consumption had bequeathed him the portrait and the false account of his intention to commit suicide. The story ends with the narrator's comment that sometimes, when he looks at the portrait, "I think there is really a great deal to be said for the Willie Hughes theory of Shakespeare's Sonnets."

The story begins, significantly, with a discussion of the literary forgeries of James MacPherson, William Ireland, and Thomas Chatterton. The narrator readily points out that ". . . we had no right to quarrel with an artist for the conditions under which he chooses to present his work; and that all Art being to a certain degree a mode of acting, an attempt to realize one's own personality on some imaginative plane out of reach of the trammeling accidents and limitations of real life, to censure an artist for a forgery was to confuse an ethical with an aesthetical problem" ("Mr. W. H.," p. 152). Thus, Wilde immediately links the critical ideas of his "Portrait of Mr. W. H." to those of *The Picture of Dorian Gray* and the essays of *Intentions*. The truth or falsity of the Willie Hughes theory of the sonnets is of little importance. What Wilde is attempting to get across is that such a "beautiful lie" serves as a powerful catalyst to creative criticism. As Erskine, one of the characters, argues, "This was Cyril Graham's theory, evolved as you see purely from the Sonnets themselves, and depending for its acceptance not so much on demonstrable proof of formal evidence, but on a kind of spiritual and artistic sense . . . (p. 160). Wilde is illustrating what he maintained later in "The Critic as Artist" that "the critic occupies the same relation to the work of art that he criticizes as the artist does to the visible world of form and colour" (I, p. 364). Criticism "does not confine itself . . . to discovering the real intention of the artist," for it is characteristic of a beautiful form that "one can put into it what one wishes" (p. 369). Willie Hughes, of course, probably never existed; but, as Wilde points out in "The Decay of Lying," "The only real people are the people who never existed" (p. 297). This is true, Wilde argues, because through the process of giving them artistic form by selection and emphasis they become more intense, more "real" than those that unselective, undiscriminating nature can give.

VII   *"The Soul of Man Under Socialism"*

"The Soul of Man Under Socialism," which appeared in *The Fortnightly Review* in 1891, is about neither the soul nor socialism.

The title, according to Hesketh Pearson, should have been "The Soul of Man Above Socialism" for the essay is mainly concerned with individualism and art.[15] In fact, there is very little that Karl Marx would have recognized. The origin of Wilde's essay was a speech on Fabian socialism given by George Bernard Shaw in Westminster, but there is little that is directly attributable to Fabian ideas.[16] The clearly expressed hostility to the idea of states and state control that Wilde expresses in his essay has more in common with anarchism. "The Soul of Man Under Socialism" reveals that Wilde, in spite of his professed hedonism and egotism, had sympathies with the mass of humanity. In this essay the flights of purple prose, the paradoxes, and the flippant tone characteristic of *Intentions* are gone. The reason for the change in style, according to Pearson, was that "For once . . . Wilde was solely concerned with what he was saying, not with how he was saying it, so he ceased to be 'literary' and wrote literature."[17]

Wilde's belief in the primacy of the individual, especially in the case of the artist, has its roots in the ideals of the English Romantics from Blake and Shelley onwards through the nineteenth century, a current which requires no documentation. No doubt a substantial debt is owed to John Stuart Mill's *On Liberty* (1859), a landmark work of the nineteenth century whose presence one cannot fail to sense in the "Critic as Artist" as well as the essay in question. The influence of Ruskin and Morris' pleas for an art with social utility is evident in Wilde's urging of meaningful creation for all men and his concern for decorative arts, although the inherent conflict of these views with Pater's that painting can have no ethical message is never resolved. The thinking of such influential teachers at Oxford as T. H. Green also should not be overlooked. Wilde's review in 1890 of a translation of the works of a Chinese Taoist anarchist *Chuang Tzu, Mystic, Moralist, and Social Reformer* was crucial. Masolino D'Amico argues that in Chuang Tzu "Wilde found a kindred spirit and probably the first suggestion towards the writing of his own social essay."[18] Chuang Tzu rejects philanthropy as useless and governments as mischievous. The ideal state of man is one of contemplative inaction, a condition certainly in harmony with Pater's aesthetics.

Ernest Renan's *L'Avenir de la Science*, written in 1848, but published in 1890, was the probable source of several salient ideas such as the belief that machinery will free man from material concerns in the future, that capitalism encourages a materialistic ethic, and that the rejection of pessimistic doctrines of human nature is necessary for social progress.[19] Other likely sources are William Godwin's *Political Justice*, Herbert Spencer's *Social Statics*, George Bernard Shaw's *Quintessence of Ibsenism*, William Morris' *News from Nowhere*, and Peter Kropotkin, the Russian anarchist whom Wilde praises in *De Profundis* for having lived one of the most perfect lives and describes as "a man with the soul of that beautiful white Christ that seems coming out of Russia" (*Letters*, p. 488).

Wilde begins with the statement that the chief advantage to be derived from the establishment of socialism would be the freeing of mankind from "that sordid necessity of living for others. . . ." Only a few privileged souls like Charles Darwin, John Keats, Ernest Renan, or Gustav Flaubert escaped this heavy burden and were able to realize the perfection that lay within them. Wilde argues that the majority of men spoil their lives by an "unhealthy and exaggerated altruism" which attempts to solve the problem of poverty by trying to keep the poor alive or "in the case of a very advanced school, by amusing the poor." Such misguided efforts are wrong because "their remedies do not cure the disease: they merely prolong it." The proper aim, on the other hand, is "to try and reconstruct society on such a basis that poverty will be impossible" ("Soul of Man Under Socialism," pp. 255-256). The altruistic virtues have prevented this aim, an idea that G. B. Shaw makes good use of in his *Major Barbara* (1905).

But Wilde's real interest in socialism does not lie in its potentialities for social betterment. According to Wilde, "*Socialism itself is of value simply because it will lead to Individualism*" ("Soul of Man Under Socialism," p. 257). In our existing society there are many who develop a limited amount of individualism. These are the poets, philosophers, scientists—men of culture—"men who have realized themselves, and in whom all Humanity gains a partial realization" ("Soul of Man Under Socialism," p. 257). But there are many who, because they have no property, are compelled to do the work of beasts of burden. Wilde grants that the virtues of the rich are not always so fine, nor are the poor without virtues. Wilde maintains that "The possession of private wealth is very often extremely demoralizing." In addition, "The virtues of the poor may be readily admitted, and are much to be regretted. We are often told that the poor are grateful for charity. Some of them are, no doubt, but the best among the poor are never grateful" ("Soul of Man

Under Socialism," p. 258). Wilde argues that it is only through disobedience, a refusal to live like a brute, that progress is ever made. In fact, a man who is ungrateful is probably a "real personality, and has much in him." As for the virtuous poor: ". . . one can pity them, of course, but one cannot possibly admire them. They have made private terms with the enemy, and sold their birthright for very bad pottage. They must also be extraordinarily stupid. I can quite understand a man accepting laws that protect private property, and admit of its accumulation, as long as he himself is able under those conditions to realize some form of beautiful and intellectual life. But it is almost incredible to me how a man whose life is marred and made hideous by such laws can possibly acquiesce in their continuance" ("Soul of Man Under Socialism," p. 259). The answer is not difficult to find, according to Wilde, for poverty is so degrading and paralyzing that no class is really conscious of its suffering. This is why outside agitators are so necessary: "Slavery was put down in America, not in consequence of any action on the part of the slaves, or even any express desire on their part that they should be free. It was put down entirely through the grossly illegal conduct of certain agitators in Boston and elsewhere, who were not slaves themselves, nor owners of slaves, nor had anything to do with the questions really" ("Soul of Man Under Socialism," p. 259).

Wilde is careful to point out that if the socialism is authoritarian and if the government instituted is "armed with economic power as they are now with political power; if, in a word, we are to have Industrial Tyrannies, then the last state of man will be worse than the first" ("Soul of Man Under Socialism," p. 260). His position on the issue of Collectivism versus Individualism distinguishes his views from Marxism. Wilde regrets that all the socialistic systems with which he has been acquainted were tainted with authority and even compulsion. To the Marxist, of course, Wilde's socialism is tainted by capitalistic individualism. To Wilde *"All modes of government are failures,"* ("Soul of Man Under Socialism," p. 266) and *"It is only in voluntary associations that man is fine"* ("Soul of Man Under Socialism," p. 260). Wilde obviously shared the socialists' dislike of capitalism, but his emphasis upon individualism has more in common with anarchism.

Wilde answers the obvious question of how individualism, presently based on the existence of private property, will benefit from the elimination of property by affirming that *"The true perfection of man lies, not in what man has, but in what man is"* ("Soul of Man Under Socialism," p. 261). Private property has generally crushed real individualism. The very effort necessary to obtain and take care of private property is demoralizing. In fact, it is questionable whether the world has ever seen the full expression of individualized personality except on the plane of art. Too much of the strength of great individuals such as Byron has been wasted in struggles with society. For Wilde the perfect realization of such a personality already existed in the person of Christ. Wilde argues that *"When Jesus talks about the poor he simply means personalities, just as when he talks about the rich he simply means people who have not developed their personalities"* ("Soul of Man Under Socialism," p. 263). Thus, the man who would lead a Christlike life is he who is perfectly and absolutely himself.

Wilde also addresses himself to the question of what the state is to do if it does not govern. Wilde's answer is that "The State is to make what is useful. The individual is to make what is beautiful" ("Soul of Man Under Socialism," p. 268). People should recognize the nonsense being written about the dignity of manual labor. Man was made for "something better than disturbing dirt. All work of that kind should be done by a machine" ("Soul of Man Under Socialism," p. 268), an idea which he no doubt derived in large part from William Morris' *News from Nowhere*. At the present time, according to Wilde, a man is a slave to his machines but this need not always be so. If machines by community organization are to make the useful things while the individual is to make beautiful things, it must be recognized that *"Art is the most intense mode of individualism that the world has known"* ("Soul of Man Under Socialism," p. 270). This individualism must never be tampered with by dictating to the artist what he should create, nor should art ever attempt to be popular. The public should make itself artistic; then it will cease asking art to flatter its own taste or conform to its own low standards. In England the arts in which the public takes no interest—poetry, for instance—have escaped the pressures to conform; but the novel and the drama, forms in which the public takes a great interest, have generally been forced to become tedious, silly, and vulgar. If such a world seems Utopian, Wilde argues, a world that does not include Utopias is not worth our concern, for "Progress is the realization of Utopias" ("Soul of Man Under Socialism," p. 270).

At the close of his essay, Wilde argues that the individualism that Christ preached, because he advocated no social changes, could be realized only through pain or solitude. Thus, Medieval Christianity with its saints and martyrs and its suffering Christ represents the world's predominating ideal of life. With the Renaissance, however, new ideals of joy and beauty in living were brought forth. The modern world, following that line of development, proposes to do away with pain and suffering:

For what man has sought for is, indeed, neither pain nor pleasure, but simply Life. Man has sought to live intensely, fully, perfectly. When he can do so without exercising restraint on others, or suffering it ever, and his activities are all pleasurable to him, he will be saner, healthier, more civilized, more himself. Pleasure is Nature's test, her sign of approval. When man is happy, he is in harmony with himself and his environment. The new Individualism, for whose service Socialism, whether it wills it or not, is working, will be perfect harmony. It will be what the Greeks sought for . . . . The new Individualism is the new Hellenism. ("Soul of Man Under Socialism," pp. 288-289)

CHAPTER 5

The Picture of Dorian Gray

The Picture of Dorian Gray, although it has certainly earned the sobriquet "literary classic," has been a troublesome book for reader and critic alike. The reader is usually fascinated by the characters, the mysterious portrait, and the only hinted-at sins of Dorian's life, but he is usually puzzled if not repelled by the tenets of the New Hedonism espoused by Wilde's characters. The critic, on the other hand, has tended to see a contradiction between the artistic credo presented in the Preface and the body of the novel and the moral significance or consequences of the events of the narrative. But when properly understood Oscar Wilde's book does possess philosophical consistency. In spite of its flaws, it succeeds as a novel.

I *Sources*

The Picture of Dorian Gray first appeared in the American *Lippincott's Magazine* in June of 1890. The novel about the Parisian that Lord Henry gives Dorian is certainly Karl Huysman's *A Rebours* (1884). The anemic, aristocratic hero of this book seeks to live a life as artistic and composed as possible. After exhausting the joys of Parisian life, he creates an artificial, isolated existence of scents, colors, tastes, and textures. No specific elements of plot are derived from *A Rebours* because Huysman's novel, comprised mostly of exposition and description, is essentially static. Nevertheless, the germ of the idea of a sensitive hero pursuing ever more intense sensuous experience certainly derives from Huysman's book. The clearest indications of Wilde's debt are found in chapter eleven of the book version where Dorian Gray most explicitly puts into practice Lord Henry's New Hedonism, whose aim was to be "experience itself, and not the fruits of experience, sweet or bitter as they might be" (*Dorian Gray,* p. 104).

Another probable French source is Honoré de Balzac's *Le Peau de Chagrin, Splendeurs et misères* (1831). In this story the hero receives as a talisman a wild ass's skin. As his wishes are granted and his desires are satisfied, the skin shrinks, thereby symbolizing the gradual destruction of the protagonist. Raphael, the main figure of Balzac's novel, watches the gradual shrinking of the skin with the same horror that Dorian watches the disfigurements of his portrait. Balzac, as H. Lucius Cook points out, was one of Wilde's favorite authors, but it cannot be maintained with any certainty that *Le Peau de Chagrin* was the direct source of *The Picture of Dorian Gray*.[1]

The most obvious and direct source of Wilde's story is, of course, the traditional Faust legend in which a man sells his soul for knowledge, experience, sensation, pleasure, and a youth with which to enjoy them. Wilde's tale, therefore, has many parallels with Goethe's *Faust* (1790). Dorian, like Faust, meets a young and innocent girl and betrays her. More significant, as Rossi argues, the girl in each of the stories is clearly playing a role for her lover and is ultimately destroyed by him.[2] Wilde himself wrote: "It takes a Goethe to see a work of art fully, completely, and perfectly . . . it is a pity that Goethe never had an opportunity of reading *Dorian Gray*" (*Letters*, p. 269).

From the vogue of the Gothic novel represented in the eighteenth century by Horace Walpole and Ann Radcliffe and culminating in the nineteenth century with Matthew Lewis, stemmed the publication in 1820 of *Melmoth the Wanderer* by Charles Maturin, Wilde's mother's uncle by marriage. Wilde was well acquainted with the novel and was proud of his literary ancestor.[3] Maturin's romance possesses a portrait of an evil ancestor who by a pact with the devil has been permitted to live one hundred and fifty years without aging. In the final pages, this evil Melmoth, who has returned to the place of his birth, suddenly ages, as Dorian does, and dies a withered old man. The portrait idea not only was familiar but was a family heirloom.

II *Plot Summary*

The Picture of Dorian Gray begins in the garden studio of Basil Hallward, a painter, with an encounter between Lord Henry Wotton, an urbane and sophisticated dandy, and Dorian Gray, a young man of exceptional personal beauty. Lord Henry is fascinated by Dorian and presents to him the tenets of his New Hedonism, whose basis is self-development leading to the perfect realization of one's nature. Obviously moved by this strange doctrine, Dorian expresses his willingness to give his soul if only the picture would grow old and he could remain forever young. Soon after this incident, he meets a young actress, Sibyl Vane, and becomes entranced by her beauty and ability to act. When she falls in love with him, she loses her ability to perform. After he cruelly rejects her, Sibyl commits suicide. At this point Dorian notices a touch of cruelty in the portrait. But Lord Henry convinces him that her death was a life-intensifying experience too marvelous to be missed and nothing more than a source of aesthetic sensation. Dorian, under Lord Henry's tutelage, pursues a secret life of pleasure and crime while the portrait reveals the progressively greater corruption of his soul. When Dorian is thirty-eight years of age, though possessing the features of a youth of twenty, he is visited by Basil, who urges him to give up his evil ways. Dorian shows Basil the now-hideous portrait and then in a fit of anger stabs him. To conceal the crime, Dorian forces Alan Campbell, a student of chemistry, whose life he has ruined, to destroy the body. One night, weeks later, Dorian tells Lord Henry that he has decided to reform his life. That evening, when he returns home to look at the portrait, he sees only a new look of cunning and hypocrisy. With a cry of anger he picks up the knife with which he stabbed Basil and plunges it into the monstrous portrait. There is a cry and then a crash. When the coachman and one of the footmen finally enter the locked room, they find a portrait "in all the wonder of his exquisite youth and beauty. Lying on the floor was a dead man, in evening dress, with a knife in his heart. He was withered, wrinkled, and loathesome of visage. It was not till they had examined the rings that they recognized who it was" (*Dorian Gray*, p. 167).

Such is the narrative of *The Picture of Dorian Gray*. A tale of definite Gothic stamp replete with the horror of murder, various unidentified secret crimes, and a touch of the supernatural. All these elements were standard in the eighteenth and nineteenth century Gothic novel. Yet, when the novel appeared in *Lippincott's* in 1890 and in book form a year later, many critics attacked it severely as an immoral work.

III   *Critical Reception*

"There is no such thing as a moral or an immoral book," Oscar Wilde wrote in his remarkable preface to the book version, "Books

are well written, or badly written. That is all" (*Dorian Gray*, p. 17).
Yet in his reply to the attack by the *St. James Gazette* upon the
earlier serialized versions he insisted that his book contained a
moral:

And the moral is this: All excess, as well as all renunciation, brings its own
punishment. The painter, Basil Hallward, worshipping physical beauty far
too much, as most painters do, dies by the hand of one in whose soul he has
created a monstrous and absurd vanity. Dorian Gray, having led a life of
mere sensation and pleasure, tries to kill conscience, and at that moment
kills himself. Lord Henry Wotton seeks to be merely the spectator of life.
He finds that those who reject the battle are more deeply wounded than
those who take part in it. Yes; there is a terrible moral in *Dorian Gray*—a
moral which the prurient will not be able to find in it, but which will be
revealed to all whose minds are healthy. Is this an artistic error? I fear it is.
It is the only error in the book. (*Letters*, p. 259)

The *St. James Gazette*, reflecting the general concern of contemporary critics with Wilde's moral stance in the book, felt that, given
the same material "Gautier could have made it romantic, entranc-
ing, beautiful. Mr. Stevenson could have made it convincing,
humorous, pathetic. . . . It has been reserved for Mr. Oscar Wilde
to make it dull and nasty." The reviewer concludes that such books
are "revelations only of the singularly unpleasant minds from which
they emerge."[4] *The Daily Chronicle* objected to the "plausibly in-
sinuated defence of the creed that appeals to the senses 'to cure the
soul' whenever the spiritual nature of man suffers from too much
purity and self-denial."[5] Wilde, in his reply to *The Daily Chronicle*,
argued that "far from wishing to emphasize any moral . . . my real
trouble . . . was that of keeping the extremely obvious moral sub-
ordinate to the artistic and romantic effect." Wilde added, "It is
poisonous if you like, but you cannot deny that it is also perfect, and
perfection is what we artists aim at" (*Letters*, pp. 263-264). Walter
Pater's favorable review in the *Bookman* is of particular interest
because the occasion of Wilde's book afforded him the opportunity
to demonstrate his moral concerns in literature—a fact often overlooked by his contemporary critics. Pater, like Wilde's detractors,
recognized in the main character of *Dorian Gray* a moral uncertainty, an inauthentic "Epicureanism": "A true Epicureanism aims
at a complete though harmonious development of man's entire or-
ganism. To lose the moral sense therefore . . . is to lose or lower
organization, to become less complex, to pass from a higher to a

lower degree of development." Thus, Pater felt the book possessed a "very plain moral, . . . to the effect that vice and crime make people coarse and ugly."[6] For Wilde's critical friends and enemies the art versus morality issue, though sometimes obscured, seemed the fundamental problem.

IV Structure

At its simplest, the structure of The Picture of Dorian Gray may be described as a variation of the Faust story in which the main character sells his soul to the devil or evil, with main portions of the novel representing the consequences of the evil pact which culminates in the protagonist's destruction. The role of Mephistopheles in Wilde's book is fulfilled by Lord Henry Wotton. The novel begins with a careful presentation of Lord Henry's credo while the remainder of the novel consists of Dorian's application of these ideas to his life.

A mythic structure is also evident in Wilde's Picture of Dorian Gray. The Garden of Eden myth with its temptation, fall, and redemption is strongly suggested. Wilde's story begins, it will be recalled, almost too obviously in a garden with an appropriately heavy emphasis upon sensuous detail: ". . . when the light summer wind stirred amidst the trees of the garden, there came through the open door the heavy scent of the lilac, or the more delicate perfume of the pink-flowering thorn" (Dorian Gray, p. 18). Equally significant is the suggestion of stasis, the scene suggesting itself to Lord Henry's finely tuned perceptions as an art that is "immobile": "The sullen murmur of the bees shouldering their way through the long unmown grass, or circling with monotonous insistence round the dusty gilt horns of the straggling woodbine, seemed to make the stillness more oppressive" (Dorian Gray, p. 18). Significantly, beyond sounded the distant "dim roar of London." At the center of this Eden stands the portrait of Dorian, perfect in its youth and purity, alone until recently with its creator Basil Hallward, who functions in a variety of ways as a moral force in the novel. The Serpent in the garden exists in the person of Lord Henry, whose first words appropriately are words of praise, which the painter rejects, for the portrait. An interesting and suggestive fact, but perhaps of less importance, is that Lord Henry, like Satan, is a gentleman, but one who emits "blue wreaths of smoke that curled up in such fanciful whorls from his heavy opium-tainted cigarette" (Dorian Gray, pp. 18-19).

Dorian, who arrives later, is described in moral terms: "There was something in his face that made one trust him at once. All the candor of youth was there, as well as all youth's passionate purity. One felt that he had kept himself unspotted from the world" (*Dorian Gray*, p. 27). Basil Hallward's portrait seems to reinforce the impression that Dorian himself has had no prior existence. There is a struggle for domination of Dorian, as Lord Henry's words indicate: "Yes! he would try to be to Dorian Gray what, without knowing it, the lad was to the painter who had fashioned the wonderful portrait. He would seek to dominate him. . . . He would make that wonderful spirit his own. There was something fascinating in this son of Love and Death" (*Dorian Gray*, p. 41). Put simply, the events in Basil's garden studio represent a temptation scene with Lord Henry offering Dorian the knowledge that will enable him to achieve self-realization.[7] What he offers Dorian is significantly interwoven with the possibility of escape from time, death, and decay by becoming a New Hedonist:

Time is jealous of you, and wars against your lilies and your roses. You will become sallow, and hollow-cheeked, and dull-eyed. You will suffer horribly. . . . Ah! realize your youth while you have it. Don't squander the gold of your days, listening to the tedious, trying to improve the hopeless failure, or giving away your life to the ignorant, the common, and the vulgar. These are the sickly aims, the false ideals, of our age. Live! Live the wonderful life that is in you! Let nothing be lost upon you. Be always searching for new sensations. Be afraid of nothing. . . . A new Hedonism—that is what our century wants. You might be its visible symbol. With your personality there is nothing you could not do. The world belongs to you for a season. . . . (*Dorian Gray*, p. 32)

Lord Henry appeals to his pride by telling him that his ". . . Beauty is a form of Genius—is higher [indeed,] than Genius" (*Dorian Gray*, p. 31). Earlier, Lord Henry had suggested that "The only way to get rid of a temptation is to yield to it." The consequence of it all is that Dorian loses his soul: "If it were I who was to be always young, and the picture that was to grow old! For that—for that—I would give everything! Yes, there is nothing in the whole world I would not give! I would give my soul for that!" (*Dorian Gray*, p. 34).

Several other parallels with the Garden of Eden myth are worthy of note. Although, in a sense, Basil Hallward is the creator of the portrait and functions as a moral voice in the book, it is Dorian himself who gradually paints the loathesome portrait. It might further be pointed out that although Lord Henry offers Dorian the dangerous knowledge of the New Hedonism, it is Dorian who fails to employ this knowledge properly and becomes corrupt. The issue of free will is important here just as it is in Milton's *Paradise Lost.* It might further be noted that it is through Sibyl Vane that Dorian first actually sins. Her function as the Eve in our myth, as her name suggests, makes it possible for the first corruption of Dorian's new knowledge to take place. Dorian makes the same error his mother made: attempting to find beauty in one who is corrupted by reality. When Sibyl confesses her love for Dorian, she, in effect, is rejecting art. Using words that echo those of Tennyson's "Lady of Shalott," she turns from life as mirrored by Art, to Life itself: "You had brought me something higher, something of which all art is but a reflection. You had made me understand what love really is. My love! my love! Prince Charming! Prince of Life! I have grown sick of shadows. You are more to me than all art can ever be" (*Dorian Gray,* p. 75). Treasonous words to any New Hedonist. Dorian appropriately, though cruelly, rejects her; but the initial error, and the error he is to repeat later, is to involve himself with what is vulgar, base, and not beautiful in his misguided search for self-realization. His sin in connection with Sibyl Vane lies not in his rejection of her, but in his failure to maintain, dare we say, "aesthetic distance" both in his initial involvement with her and in his rejection. Basil himself confesses to the same error. Only Lord Henry escapes it for he knows that "To become the spectator of one's own life . . . is to escape the suffering of life" (*Dorian Gray,* p. 91).

The Adonis-Narcissus myth also appears to permeate the structure of the novel.[8] Lord Henry describes Dorian in such terms in the first chapter in response to Basil's expression of regret for having put too much of himself into the portrait: "Upon my word, Basil, I didn't know you were so vain; and I really can't see any resemblance between you . . . and this young Adonis, who looks as if he was made out of ivory and rose-leaves. Why, my dear Basil, he is a Narcissus . . ." (*Dorian Gray,* p. 19). Just as Adonis is traditionally described, so Dorian is "wonderfully handsome, with his finely-curved scarlet lips, his frank blue eyes, his crisp gold hair" (*Dorian Gray,* p. 27). Appropriately his artistic preferences are for forests. At the opening of chapter two he expresses a desire to learn Schuman's "Forest Scenes" (*Dorian Gray,* p. 27). After hearing one of Sibyl's performances he exclaims: "I forgot that I was in London and in the nineteenth century. I was away with my love in a forest that no man had ever seen" (*Dorian Gray*, p. 67). This motif culminates in the accidental shooting of James Vane. Like the huntsman in the Adonis story, Dorian says "The grass of the forest had been spotted with blood." Dorian recognizes in James Vane's death the possible end of his own life: "I have a horrible presentiment that something of the kind may happen to me" (*Dorian Gray*, p. 154). Several such seasonal references reinforce this Adonis-Narcissus motif. In the myth of Adonis the gods decreed that he was to have a divided existence, living six months with mankind during spring and summer and six months with the gods during fall and winter. By means of the portrait Dorian escapes the cycles of time and aging which this myth suggests. Through Dorian's conversion of life into Art, however ultimately faulty, he escapes time.

Although the two mythic patterns mentioned—the Garden of Eden-temptation and Adonis-Narcissus myths—are not fully developed nor always fully consistent with Wilde's ideas in *The Picture of Dorian Gray*, they supply a mythic substructure to the plot that vastly enriches the narrative and represents one of the fundamental reasons for the success of the book. It must be added, however, that many of the long-standing critical difficulties stem from Wilde's superimposing upon these myths his own set of critical ideas. The critics of his own time were not prepared for such audacious tampering with tradition.

V *Characterization*

"Basil Hallward is what I think I am: Lord Henry what the world thinks of me: Dorian what I would like to be—in other ages, perhaps" (*Letters*, p. 352). Thus, Wilde wrote of his main characters in a letter dated 1894. Although it is interesting to speculate upon the degree of truth in Wilde's well-known letter, it is probably of slight importance to our understanding of *The Picture of Dorian Gray* for, if it were important to link the author with any one of these characters, we should probably fail for there is much of Wilde in each of them. Nevertheless, such a provocative statement by an author immediately stimulates the reader to speculate whether all three men represent portraits of the author with differing degrees of resemblance or if, indeed, one can trust the author at all. Roditi, in fact, argues that in Basil, we find "the embodiment of the conscience which later prevented Wilde from escaping abroad to avoid arrest at the time of his trials, and which then dictated to him many of the penitent passages of *De Profundis.*" He further suggests that, psychoanalytically, "Dorian," Wilde's id, "is driven to self-inflicted death by his misinterpreting . . . the doctrines of beauty and pleasure . . . preached by Lord Henry, Wilde's Ego; and that Basil, the author's Super-Ego, is killed when his warnings and reproaches might frustrate Dorian in his unbridled pursuit of sensual satisfactions."[9] This observation, offered only tentatively by Roditi, has perhaps more symmetry than significance, for the real issues reside in the relationship of each of these characters to Wilde's theories of art and criticism.

Dorian Gray at first glance seems to be the protagonist of the action. But he rarely becomes anything more than a mechanical device to illustrate Wilde's ideas. He exists mainly as a quiveringly sensitive medium for Lord Henry's shaping hands. He is mainly acted upon in the sense that the basic motives for his life of pleasure stem from Lord Henry, who sets out to dominate him: "Yes; he would try to be to Dorian Gray what, without knowing it, the lad was to the painter who had fashioned the wonderful portrait. He would seek to dominate him—had already, indeed, half done so. He would make that wonderful spirit his own" (*Dorian Gray,* p. 41). To Lord Henry, Dorian appears to exist as nothing more than a "green bronze figure"—some gracious form: "To project one's soul into some gracious form, and let it tarry there for a moment; to hear one's own intellectual views echoed back to one with all the added music of passion and youth; to convey one's temperament into another as though it were a subtle fluid or a strange perfume: there was a real joy in that—perhaps the most satisfying joy left to us in an age so limited and vulgar as our own" (*Dorian Gray,* p. 41). Because Dorian is not the source of the ideas which activate him, he is basically a static character. Dorian's static nature derives in large part from Wilde's deliberate withholding of information about his background. One feels, as Lord Henry observed, "that he had kept himself unspotted from the world" (*Dorian Gray,* p. 27). Although Lord Henry learns that Dorian is the offspring of "a strange, modern romance" of "a beautiful woman risking everything for a mad passion," a passion "cut short by a hideous, treacherous crime," we learn nothing of the effects of all this upon this sensitive young man. But to provide Dorian with a personality already shaped by prior experiences would not have been consistent with the idea of the apprenticeship novel nor Wilde's other fictional purposes.

Basil Hallward is similarly flat and undeveloped for he seems to have no private existence beyond his studio. His major function is to serve as a foil for Lord Henry, for Basil's moral sensibilities stand in sharp contrast to Lord Henry's. The personal viewpoints of Basil Hallward and Lord Henry are strongly suggestive, as Richard Ellmann indicates, of the contrasting judgments concerning aesthetic taste and moral and social values associated with John Ruskin and Walter Pater.[10] Basil in chapter twelve speaks to Dorian of the widespread rumor of his crimes. He speaks of the effects of immorality upon society and upon the doer. Both concepts of the effects of sin are fallacious in Lord Henry's view. The notion that art is involved with life or that it exists as something separate lies at the heart of the differences between the two characters. Basil gives himself to life. Although this position corresponds to society's view, it leads him into difficulties. Basil confesses his error to Lord Henry: "There is too much of myself in the thing [the portrait], Harry—too much of myself" (*Dorian Gray*, p. 25). Hallward violates his own artistic precept that "An artist should create beautiful things, but should put nothing of his own life into them. We live in an age when men treat art as if it were meant to be a form of autobiography. We have lost the abstract sense of beauty" (*Dorian Gray*, p. 25). The consequence of such involvement in life, as Lord Henry points out later in the novel, is that Basil's work has become "that curious mixture of bad painting and good intentions that always entitles a man to be called a representative British artist" (*Dorian Gray*, p. 161). Although Basil is an artist, he is not an artist of life, but one who makes *objets d'art*, who prefers the ideal of reality, for he tells Dorian and Lord Henry that "Love is a more wonderful thing than Art" (*Dorian Gray*, p. 73). As Baker suggests, "Hallward's initial self-consciousness and mishandling of the ideal have doleful consequences, and it is significant that the artist himself introduces Dorian to Lord Henry."[11] Although the significance of this introduction is lessened by Hallward's reluctance to make the introduction and the chance arrival of Dorian at the studio, the chain of events that Baker points out—the self-consciousness of the artist, the corruption of the ideal, and the hedonistic pursuit of exquisite sensation—does suggest that Hallward sets the entire sequence in motion. However, his function as an activator of the plot is of less importance than his idolatry of Dorian which undermines his artistic beliefs.

Although characterization never interested Oscar Wilde, he did make one distinct contribution in the sophisticated dandy who inhabits his novel and most of his plays. In *The Picture of Dorian Gray* it is clear that the bulk of Wilde's creative energies are expended in the delineation of Lord Henry Wotton. The result is that Lord Henry is the most interesting character in the book. Furthermore, he is the real protagonist of the action. Whereas Dorian seems merely acted upon, Lord Henry influences action although he never acts and he never changes. Lord Henry is given the task of expounding the doctrines of the New Hedonism and consequently gets all the best lines.

Lord Henry is the fascinating embodiment of the *fin de siècle* dandy. He is languid in his postures and movements yet his exquisitely attuned senses never miss sensory impressions such as "the sullen murmur of bees shouldering their way through the long unmown grass" nor how "like a blue thread a long thin dragon-fly floated past on its brown gauze wings." He smokes "opium-tainted" cigarettes ceaselessly. He is intimate with the rich, talented, and well-born and is a connoisseur of all the arts. Lord Henry is an artist of life and his brilliant witticisms that abound in the book, though their artificial inversions of conventional morality amuse rather than convince, are examples of what Wilde calls a "truth in Art . . . whose contradictory is also true."

Lord Henry is an artist in the highest Wildean sense. Although he is not the creator of objects of art, he has succeeded in creating the new artistic personality in Dorian Gray:

> . . . the lad was his own creation. He had made him premature. That was something. Ordinary people waited till life disclosed to them its secrets, but to the few, to the elect, the mysteries of life were revealed before the veil was drawn away. Sometimes this was the effect of art, and chiefly of the art of literature, which dealt immediately with the passions and the intellect. But now and then a complex personality took the place and assumed the office of art; was indeed, in its way, a real work of art, Life having its elaborate masterpieces, just as poetry has, or sculpture, or painting. (*Dorian Gray*, p. 55)

Lord Henry sees himself as a creative artist no less than Basil Hallward: "Yes; he would try to be to Dorian Gray what, without knowing it, the lad was to the painter who had fashioned the wonderful portrait" (*Dorian Gray*, p. 41). Dorian becomes the creation of Lord Henry. When Lord Henry first meets Dorian the young man seems to have no past that could have shaped him. Hence, he is the perfect medium for the artist of personality. At certain crisis points, Lord Henry guides the young hedonist. Appropriately, when Sibyl Vane poisons herself after Dorian's rejection of her, it is Lord Henry who provides the consolation:

> It often happens that the real tragedies of life occur in such an inartistic manner that they hurt us by their crude violence, their absolute incoherence, their absurd want of meaning, their entire lack of style. . . . Sometimes, however, a tragedy that possesses artistic elements of beauty crosses our lives. If these elements of beauty are real, the whole thing simply appeals to our sense of dramatic effect. Suddenly we find that we are no longer the actors, but the spectators of the play. Or rather we are both. (*Dorian Gray*, p. 84)

Dorian learns from Lord Henry that "To become the spectator of one's own life . . . is to escape the suffering of life" (*Dorian Gray*, p. 91). Dorian learns that "Life itself was the first, the greatest, of the arts, and for it all the other arts seemed to be but a preparation" (*Dorian Gray*, p. 103). Such detachment is a necessary condition for art, for the aim of the New Hedonism was to be "experience itself, and not the fruits of experience" (*Dorian Gray*, p. 104). Such an approach to life as art would reject the ascetic or the puritanical and reach for any passionate experience that would refine the personality. Whether by the artist's detachment from experience and his rejection of conventional standards of morality he becomes insincere is of no importance, for insincerity "is merely a method by which we can multiply our personalities" (*Dorian Gray*, p. 112).

At the end of the novel Lord Henry's final assessment of his creation is unstinted: "Ah, Dorian, how happy you are! What an exquisite life you have had! You have drunk deeply of everything. You have crushed the grapes against your palate. Nothing has been hidden from you. And it has all been to you no more than the sound of music. It has not marred you. You are still the same" (*Dorian Gray*, p. 162). Dorian denies that he is unchanged, but Lord Henry denies any flaws in his creation in spite of the world's possible judgments: "The world has cried out against us both, but it has always worshipped you. It always will worship you. You are the type of what the age is searching for, and what it is afraid it has found. I am so glad that you have never done anything—never carved a statue, or painted a picture, or produced anything outside of yourself! Life has been your art. You have set yourself to music. Your days are your sonnets" (*Dorian Gray*, p. 163). Dorian agrees that life has been exquisite but, nevertheless, insists that his manner of life is going to change. To Dorian's accusation that he was poisoned by the book that he had loaned him, Lord Henry replies that "there is no such thing as that. Art has no influence upon action" (*Dorian Gray*, p. 163). In short, Lord Henry sees his work of art as complete and without flaws.

Sibyl Vane, even by contrast with Dorian and Lord Henry, seems almost totally lacking in psychological reality. But her authentic existence as a character is not of great importance because she serves mainly to represent an idea. When Dorian professes his love, he is professing a love not for Sibyl Vane but for the art forms she is capable of creating: "Why should I not love her? Harry, I do love her. She is everything to me in life. . . . One evening she is Rosalind, and the next evening she is Imogen. I have seen her die in the gloom of an Italian tomb, sucking the poison from her lover's lips. . . . I have seen her in every age and in every costume. Ordinary women never appeal to one's imagination. They are limited to their century. No glamour ever transfigures them" (*Dorian Gray*, p. 51). When Dorian finally meets her he is struck that she regarded him "merely as a person in a play" (*Dorian Gray*, p. 53). She seemed to know nothing of life and Dorian finds that he has no interest in her past. When Lord Henry asks Dorian when his new love exists as the real Sibyl Vane, Dorian replies "Never."

Sibyl, of course, never understands why her "Prince Charming," as she calls him, can love someone so far beneath him. When Dorian explains his love in Pateresque terms to Basil the artist, he reveals the real object of his devotion: "She is simply a born artist. I sat in the dingy box absolutely enthralled. I forgot that I was in London, and in the nineteenth century. I was away with my love in a forest that no man had ever seen. After the performance was over I went behind, and spoke to her. As we were sitting together, suddenly there came into her eyes a look that I had never seen there before. My lips moved towards hers. We kissed each other. I can't describe to you what I felt at that moment. It seemed to me that all my life had been narrowed to one perfect point of rose-colored joy" (*Dorian Gray*, p. 67). To Dorian, Sibyl exists only as an artist who takes what is "coarse and brutal" in her audience and in reality and spiritualizes it in the form of art. Wilde takes great care to emphasize her lower-class origin but stresses the ideal nature of her beauty: "Through the crowd of ungainly, shabbily dressed actors, Sibyl Vane moved like a creature from a finer world. Her body swayed, while she danced, as a plant sways in the water. The curves of her throat were the curves of a white lily. Her hands seemed to be made of cool ivory" (*Dorian Gray*, p. 72).

By setting the perfection of her beauty against the sordidness of her surroundings, Wilde suggests a relationship between art and life similar to the one he presents in "The Critic as Artist." After dismissing most modern art as "just a little less vulgar than reality" he argues that the critic: ". . . with his fine sense of distinction and sure instinct of delicate refinements, will prefer to look into the silver mirror or through the woven veil, and will turn his eyes away from the chaos and clamour of actual existence, though the mirror be tarnished and the veil be torn" ("The Critic as Artist," pp. 365-66). Significantly, when Sibyl falls in love with Dorian, her confession of love horrifies Dorian because of its obvious rejection of his artistic credo: "Dorian, Dorian . . . before I knew you, acting was the one reality of my life. . . . You had brought me something higher, something of which all art is but a reflection. . . . I have grown sick of shadows. You are more to me than all art can ever be" (*Dorian Gray*, p. 74). When Dorian hears this inadvertent denial of his ideal, he cruelly rejects her. Sibyl, like the Lady of Shalott, whose words she echoes, dies because she gives herself to life rather than to Art.[12] Significantly, the pain of Dorian's loss is later softened by the infusion of beauty into his life, in this case, by the scent and form of flowers as he wanders the streets at night in distress.

Sibyl's mother and James Vane in related ways illustrate the same motif. Mrs. Vane, an unpleasant woman living in meager circumstances, escapes the sordid reality of her existence by transforming it into a bearable form with melodramatic gestures and lines from old plays, thus reinforcing Wilde's ideas concerning the relationship of art and reality. James Vane, the brother, on the other hand, appears to represent the reality, sordid or otherwise, which ever more closely impinges on Dorian—a reality that is associated with society and conventional morality. We are not allowed to feel much, if any, sympathy for him for he is usually rendered with brutal detail. He reveals no sensitivity, just a sense of justice based on the most primitive revenge morality. His appearance in the novel coincides with the general revelation of Dorian's own abasement by an increasing fascination with the ugly and the sordid. It is significant that they meet outside the opium den at the waterfront.

VI *Imagery, Language, and Setting*

The Picture of Dorian Gray, with the exception of the hunt scene in the later portion of the novel, takes place in an urban setting. Basil's studio, Dorian's attic room, Sibyl's dressing room, a conservatory, a waterfront opium den, Lord Fermor's house, the tiny Picadilly theater, the various dining rooms—represent a sharply confined urban world. The physical setting, though urban, is replete with associated images of birds, clouds, breezes, sunlight, and natural scents and sounds.[13] But these images are perceived by the characters, except when under stress, in a manner that suggests a refined, highly selective perceiving mind. This is not accidental, for Wilde's purpose in using such restricted settings is to convey a sense of limitation, stasis, and conscious form in order to realize one of the dominant motifs in the novel: that through art the welter and flux of life experience is given form and beauty. Thus, Jan Gordon argues that "The spatial configuration of *The Picture of Dorian Gray*, for which the above scene is an analogue, presents us with an inversion of many commonly-held nineteenth century attitudes about the relationship between art and the world from which art is made."[14] Gordon's argument that the fact that the portrait ages while the artist remains immutable represents an inversion is, in a limited sense, correct. But the fundamental relationship—between the artist of life and/or the work of art and the mutable world beyond from whose raw materials the artist creates his form—remains uninverted. The stasis of form embodied in Dorian is what any artist strives for. Hence, there is no real inversion, for Dorian is the art work; the portrait is mutable reality. The equation is the same, only the terms have been changed. Wilde suggests this by imagery that contrasts a setting given form by the shaping, limiting effect of art with a world of raw, undigested sense data. The opening scene in Basil's studio introduces this motif:

The studio was filled with the rich odor of roses, and when the light summer wind stirred amidst the trees of the garden, there came through the open door the heavy scent of the lilac, or the more delicate perfume of the pink-flowering thorn.

    From the corner of the divan of Persian saddle-bags on which he was lying, smoking, as was his custom, innumerable cigarettes, Lord Henry

Wotton could just catch the gleam of the honey-sweet and honey-colored blossoms of a laburnum, whose tremulous branches seemed hardly able to bear the burden of a beauty so flame-like as theirs; and now and then the fantastic shadows of birds in flight flitted across the long tussore-silk curtains that were stretched in front of the huge window, producing a kind of momentary Japanese effect, and making him think of those pallid jade-faced painters of Tokio who, through the medium of an art that is necessarily immobile, seek to convey the sense of swiftness and motion. The sullen murmur of the bees shouldering their way through the long unmown grass, or circling with monotonous insistence round the dusty gilt horns of the straggling woodbine, seemed to make the stillness more oppressive. The dim roar of London was like the bourdon note of a distant organ. (*Dorian Gray*, p. 18)

The scene is a striking illustration of what Wilde describes as "mind expressing itself under the conditions of matter" ("The Critic as Artist," II, p. 382). The shaping mind, as the point-of-view of the passage reveals, is Lord Henry's. A wide variety of sensuous detail is provided whose cumulative effect of a fleeting beauty suggests an art "necessarily immobile" like that of the Japanese painters. One of the striking ways that Wilde conveys his impressions of the artistic personality is by revealing the intense awareness of sensory details. But beyond the shaping critical spirit of Lord Henry and the idyllic garden studio "the dim roar of London was like the bourdon note of a distant organ."

On other occasions a different sort of imagery is employed to suggest the same motif. Dorian rejects Sibyl, who has rejected Art fot the reality of her love. Dorian, having lost his love, the Sibyl who existed only as a form of art, leaves the theater and goes out into the streets and chaotic reality:

He remembered wandering through dimly-lit streets, past gaunt black-shadowed archways and evil-looking houses. Women with hoarse voices and harsh laughter had called after him. Drunkards had reeled by cursing, and chattering to themselves like monstrous apes. He had seen grotesque children huddled upon doorsteps, and heard shrieks and oaths from gloomy courts. (*Dorian Gray*, p. 76)

The abundance of images that suggest distortion of form, i.e., "gaunt, black-shadowed archways," "evil-looking houses," "hoarse voices," "harsh laughter," "monstrous apes," "grotesque children," is significant for it suggests the chaos that exists without Art. Appropriately, this welter of sensory impressions of the shapelessness of reality is dissipated by the restored artistic perception of Dorian of the dawn when "the sky hallowed itself into a perfect pearl" and he is further eased by a flower cart filled with lilies whose perfume and beauty "seemed to bring him an anodyne for his pain" (*Dorian Gray*, p. 76).

Throughout the novel lavish and ornate descriptions are balanced by such grotesque descriptions in order to contrast artistic order and harmony with the flux and chaos of reality. Color is used in a similar manner, as Gordon suggests, to indicate the organizing mental process of the imaginative artist in contrast with the gray, undifferentiated world of the Philistines.[15] The intensification of such imagery of grayness, darkness, and somberness increases as the story nears its end.

Such passages reinforce brilliantly the major artistic theme of the novel, but they also are Expressionistic in that they represent the shaping of objective reality in order to convey the mental states of various characters. It is apparent, as critics have noted, that Wilde uses a kind of stream-of-consciousness technique where such Expressionistic emphases are most common.[16] The aftermath of Dorian's rejection of Sibyl, Dorian's journey to the waterfront, and the opening scene in Basil's garden studio illustrate this technique. When James Vane, distressed over Sibyl's confession of her love and annoyed by the prospect of enduring his mother's scenes, sits down to his meager meal: "The flies buzzed round the table, and crawled over the stained cloth. Through the rumble of omnibuses, and the clatter of street-cabs, he could hear the droning voice devouring each minute that was left to him" (*Dorian Gray*, p. 64). Unpleasant aspects of reality such as the sordidness of his home and the cacophonous outside world of London are intensified by James' unrest. When Dorian is most fearful of the possible consequences of James Vane's suspicions: "The dead leaves that were blown against the leaded panes seemed to him like his own wasted resolutions and wild regrets" (*Dorian Gray*, p. 151). When Dorian is driving across the park to join the shooting party: "The crisp frost lay like salt upon the grass. The sky was an inverted cup of blue metal. A thin film of ice bordered the flat reed-grown lake" (*Dorian Gray*, p. 152). Dorian's deteriorating artistic personality as well as his psychological state-of-mind are brilliantly conveyed in such passages.

VII *Problems of Interpretation*

The Picture of Dorian Gray succeeds as a work of art because of the originality of its narrative, the brilliant exploitation of the Gothic form, the effective fusion of language with character and idea, and the creation in Dorian and Lord Henry of original characters. But *The Picture of Dorian Gray*, in spite of its success, provides many problems of interpretation. The fundamental difficulty stems from the apparent tendency of the novel to look two ways. The tone of the novel suggests approval of the New Hedonism, yet the events, particularly the ending, suggest its condemnation. Dorian himself never repents of his actions. Lord Henry, who is certainly responsible for Dorian's strange life, never is punished nor regrets his influence.

The function of the portrait is equally obscure. Does it represent Dorian's soul, his conscience, or something else? If the portrait represents Dorian's soul, why does it return to its original purity after Dorian's death? Surely Dorian has never repented or been purified in any way. If it represents his conscience, as Dorian says, what moral significance resides in Dorian's destruction of it and its subsequent return to its original state? If Lord Henry's aesthetic principles are true, and they correspond perfectly with Wilde's expressed artistic credo in his prose works, why does the portrait become ugly?

The answer to most, if not all, of these problems lies in the correct reading of the artistic/critical message of *The Picture of Dorian Gray*. Any ethical message, therefore, must be based on Wilde's artistic credo. To Wilde, "Form is the beginning of things," and "critical and cultured spirits" like Dorian Gray but much more so Lord Henry Wotton "will seek to gain their impressions almost entirely from what Art has touched. For Life is terribly deficient in form" ("Critic as Artist," II, p. 372). This is precisely what the central figures in Wilde's novel are attempting to do—create form out of a chaotic reality.[17] But Dorian's efforts to escape the laws of time and contingency are only a part of the novel's point. Lord Henry, Basil Hallward, and even Sibyl Vane, in a special sense, each illustrates a "life that has for its aim not *doing* but *being*, and not being merely, but *becoming*" ("Critic as Artist," II, p. 384). But each fails to impart to his own life the aesthetic form that the proper critical spirit makes possible. Roditi comes closest to recognizing this principle operating in the novel when he argues that Lord Henry, who expounds this doctrine to Dorian, never falls because he never acts. But Dorian "in the passion of his self-love . . . distorts this doctrine and becomes a fallen dandy, corrupting all those who accompany him along his path and murdering his conscience, Basil Hallward."[18]

The course of Dorian's corruption is easily illustrated. When Dorian fell in love with Sibyl he fell in love not with the real person but the art she created. Dorian is unable at this point in his development to make this distinction readily. Thus, his decision to marry Sibyl is not, as San Juan suggests, a betrayal of his true nature.[19] He is reaching out for beauty and thus acting in harmony with his innermost self and Lord Henry's principles. He does, as San Juan argues, succumb to "sensual dissipation" and "a passionate indifference which makes him incapable of feeling compassion for others."[20] But Dorian, by fixing his affections on the real person, becomes dangerously enmeshed in sordid life. As Wilde himself argued, "My story is an essay on decorative art. It reacts against the crude brutality of plain realism" (*Letters*, p. 264). To represent what is outside of the proper sphere of the artist/critic, except as material for his art, is the function of the Vane family. Dorian fails to maintain detachment. In "The Decay of Lying," Wilde explains this relationship between Art and Life:

Art takes life as part of her rough material, recreates it, and refashions it in fresh forms, is absolutely indifferent to fact, invents, imagines, dreams, and keeps between herself and reality the impenetrable barrier of beautiful style, of decorative or ideal treatment. . . . when life gets the upper hand, and drives Art out into the wilderness. This is the true decadence. . . . ("Decay of Lying," p. 301)

Dorian comes dangerously close to such "decadence"; and, in reaction to Sibyl, who allows Life to get the upper hand, he responds with a cruelty and ugliness appropriate to that condition when life momentarily "gets the upper hand." Thus, at this time the first degeneration is revealed in the portrait. But Dorian is restored by beauty.

What ought to be life dedicated to art and beauty becomes through self-love mere self-gratification. This Dorian himself recognizes at the end of the novel when he confesses to Lord Henry that the personality that he has fashioned under Lord Henry's tutelage has "become a burden": ". . . I seem to have lost the passion, and forgotten the desire. I am too much concentrated on myself" (*Dorian Gray*, p. 154). Dorian earlier in the novel accuses Basil of responsibility for his degeneration: "You are the one man in the world who is entitled to know everything about me. You have had more to do with my life than you think." A few moments before Dorian murders Basil, he crushes in his hand a flower, suggestive of the life of true beauty that has been marred, and cries, "you met me, flattered me, and taught me to be vain of my good looks. One day you introduced me to a friend of yours, who explained to me the wonder of youth, and you finished a portrait of me that revealed to me the wonder of beauty. In a mad moment . . . I made a wish . . ." (*Dorian Gray*, p. 121). The form of Dorian's life continues to degenerate until at the close of the book:

Ugliness that had once been hateful to him because it made things real, became dear to him now for that very reason. Ugliness was the one reality. The coarse brawl, the loathsome den, the crude violence of disordered life, the very vileness of thief and outcast, were more vivid, in their intense actuality of impression, than all the gracious shapes of Art, the dreamy shadows of Song. (*Dorian Gray*, p. 141)

From Wilde's critical standpoint, no greater betrayal of the critical spirit could be possible. Dorian, by allowing "Life to get the upper hand," becomes a true decadent. The portrait, then, becomes not the record of his sin or his conscience, but of his artistic decadence. When he ceases to be a spectator of life and becomes enmeshed in the mundane realities of self-gratification and crime, his life and personality cease to be art, and the suspension of time which is art's great gift finally ends.

Basil Hallward, although another sort of artist, also fails. When Basil explains to Lord Henry his fascination with the young Dorian, he has already lost the proper artistic stance in relation to his subject: "I knew that I had come face to face with some one whose mere personality was so fascinating that, if I allowed it to do so, it would absorb my whole nature, my whole soul, my very art itself. I did not want any external influence in my life. . . . I have always been my own master" (*Dorian Gray*, p. 21). Basil's friendship with Dorian has had a salutary effect upon his art. Basil points out that "Dorian Gray is to me simply a motive in art. . . . He is never more present in my work than when no image of him is there" (*Dorian Gray*, p. 24). This is in keeping with Wilde's artistic credo, for Basil several passages later argues that "An artist should create beautiful things, but should put nothing of his own life into them" (*Dorian Gray*, p. 25). What is often overlooked is the fact that Basil is referring to the art created before the portrait was attempted in a new style of art:

One day, a fatal day I sometimes think, I determined to paint a wonderful portrait of you as you actually are, not in the costume of dead ages, but in your own dress and in your own time. Whether it was the Realism of the method, or the mere wonder of your own personality, thus directly presented to me without mist or veil, I cannot tell. But I know that as I worked at it, every flake and film of color seemed to me to reveal my secret. I grew afraid that others would know of my idolatry. I felt, Dorian, that I had told too much, that I had put too much of myself into it. (*Dorian Gray*, p. 94)

The portrait, in other words, represents bad art, just as Wilde maintained in "The Decay of Lying," "All bad art comes from returning to life and nature, and elevating them into ideals" ("Decay of Lying," p. 319). This is precisely Basil's error and the error he himself recognizes. Since the creation of the portrait Basil's work had become, in Lord Henry's judgment, that "curious mixture of bad painting and good intentions" (*Dorian Gray*, p. 161) characteristic of British art. Lord Henry is simply restating here Wilde's dictum in "The Critic as Artist" that "the sphere of Art and the sphere of Ethics are absolutely distinct and separate. When they are confused Chaos has come again" ("Critic as Artist," II, p. 393).

The portrait then represents neither soul nor conscience but art.[21] Its degeneration is analogous to the progressive degeneration or corruption of the ideal of the artistic personality, another form of art, which Dorian attempts to create under Lord Henry's tutelage. Just as Basil creates a portrait tainted by realism and self-involvement, so Lord Henry creates an artistic personality ultimately debased by reality and self-love. Thus, Dorian's portrait serves as a scapegoat for a life of art that succumbs increasingly to vulgar self-gratification. Only Lord Henry escapes the pitfalls of the New Hedonism. As the true critic and artist, his personality never becomes a burden to him, for the artistic form Lord Henry created in his own life and personality is held separate from life and consequently never degenerates into chaos.

The reader who is unfamiliar with Wilde's artistic credo has difficulty reconciling Lord Henry's emergence unscathed after seducing Dorian into the doctrines of the New Hedonism. But the problem stems from the tendency of readers to see Dorian as fulfilling Lord Henry's credo. This he most certainly does not do. The New Hedonism, though dangerous, is not inherently immoral. Wilde does not approve of Dorian's life for it violates all the principles of his artistic credo.[22] Wilde's mistakes, as he admits in his letter to the editor of the *St. James Gazette*, were "that it [the novel] is far too crowded with sensational incident, and far too paradoxical in style, as far, at any rate, as the dialogue goes." Wilde is quite correct. The events of the book do not contradict Wilde's own preface, as Alick West argues,[23] nor is it an uncommitted work as Jacob Korg maintains.[24] On the contrary, the events of the narrative, the imagery and setting, and the ideas expressed and objectified by the characters are in harmony with the artistic message Wilde sets forth in his critical writings and in his preface.

CHAPTER 6

The Drama

WRITING to Lord Alfred Douglas in 1897, Wilde summed up his contributions to drama: "If I were asked of myself as a dramatist, I would say that my unique position was that I had taken the Drama, the most objective form known to art, and made it as personal a mode of expression as the Lyric or the Sonnet, while enriching the characterization of the stage, and enlarging—at any rate in the case of *Salome*—its artistic horizon" (*Letters*, p. 589). Wilde does not overrate his contributions to the drama. In *The Importance of Being Earnest* he created the finest English comedy since Richard Brinsley Sheridan's *School for Scandal*. In *Earnest*, and to a lesser extent in the three earlier comedies, Wilde brought a quality of elegance, wit, and sparkle that English drama had lacked for over a century. With *Salome*, as Wilde himself realized, he created a new kind of drama that united symbol, poetic language and rhythms, physical atmosphere, and character into a single dramatic statement. The artistic horizons that Wilde felt he had enlarged were to have a substantial shaping influence upon the Symbolist drama of no less a figure than W. B. Yeats.[1] The society comedies, on the other hand, look forward to the lighter drama of Somerset Maugham and Noel Coward in the twentieth century. In the view of some critics, Wilde's concern for the absurdities of language and situation in these comedies looks ahead to the Absurdist plays of Eugene Ionesco and Samuel Beckett.[2]

I Vera: Or the Nihilists

Wilde's first play is a melodramatic love story that has its setting in the pre-revolutionary political and ideological turmoils of Czarist Russia. "Nihilism," the belief that the destruction of existing political or social institutions is necessary to insure future improvement, was a popular topic in England in the early part of 1880 when Oscar

118

Wilde wrote his first play. When Czar Alexander II, the liberator in 1861 of many millions of Russian serfs, was assassinated in March of 1881 in St. Petersburg, interest in Russia and its political turmoils increased even more. No doubt Wilde felt his play stood a solid chance of popular success. He found a producer and a leading lady for a production scheduled for December 17, 1881, at the Adelphi Theatre. However, the opening was cancelled with an announcement in the *World* that "considering the present state of political feeling in England, Mr. Oscar Wilde has decided on postponing, for a time, the production of his drama, *Vera*."[3] But the real reason, according to Pearson, lay in the fact that the Czar's wife was the sister-in-law of the Prince of Wales, a social leader and admirer of Wilde.[4] Oscar was much too kind and discreet to offend such a well-known figure. The play was finally produced in New York on August 20. The response, in spite of such Wildean touches as the yellow satin council chamber and Marie Prescott's vivid vermilion dress, was less than enthusiastic. The *New York Times*, although it admitted a "great deal of good writing in *Vera*," dismissed it as "unreal, long-winded, and wearisome."[5] The play ran for only one week. Wilde, who had come to New York for the opening, left for England in September to be greeted on his arrival with the observation in *Punch* that *Vera* was "from all accounts, except the Poet's own, Vera Bad."[6]

Vera: Or the Nihilists is a play about a Russian peasant girl who, after her brother is exiled to Siberia, becomes the leader of a group of underground Nihilists in Moscow. Alexis, a young medical student but in reality the son of the Czar, is in love with Vera. He is accused of being a traitor by Michael, a ruthless Nihilist, who once loved Vera. Alexis saves the group as they are about to be arrested by revealing his identity to the police. When the Czar is assassinated by Michael, Alexis takes the throne and attempts to reform the country. He exiles a ruthless Count Paul Maraloffski, the major cause of the oppression of the dead Czar's regime. Later the Count joins the Nihilist group and convinces them that Alexis must be assassinated. Vera is designated as assassin and is instructed to signal the completion of her task by throwing the dagger from the palace window. Vera slips into the unguarded palace and is about to stab Alexis when he awakens and convinces her that his love supersedes her vows. She relents but the clock strikes midnight and the sounds of her co-conspirators are heard. Vera stabs herself in order to save him and throws the bloody dagger from the window crying "I have saved Russia."

Vera is a play that suffers from a variety of dramatic deficiencies. Dimitri's sudden appearance in chains in the Prologue, the double life of the Czar's son as both Czarevitch and Nihilist, and the ready acceptance by the Nihilists of Prince Paul, the oppressive former prime minister, all are examples of some of the improbabilities that mar the play. More serious flaws are revealed by the following lines from the second act:

> Czar: O God! My own son against me, my own flesh and
> blood against me; but I am rid of them all now.
> Czarevitch: The mighty brotherhood to which I belong has
> a thousand such as I am, ten thousand better still! (The Czar
> starts in his seat.) The star of freedom is risen
> already, and far off I hear the mighty wave Democracy
> break on these cursed shores.
> Prince Paul: In that case you and I must learn how to swim.
> (*Vera*, p. 672)

The intended seriousness of the situation, already marred by Wilde's high-flown rhetoric, is further undercut by Prince Paul's flippant rejoinder which seems to play upon the inflated rhetoric. These two problems, the failure to control language and inconsistency of tone, plagued Wilde's drama up until he wrote *The Importance of Being Earnest*.

In spite of its glaring imperfections, *Vera: Or the Nihilists* anticipates much of the best in Wildean drama. Present at this first stage of Wilde's development is a good sense of what constitutes good theater. Each of the acts is well organized, has a powerful climax, and leads inevitably to the next. Moreover, there is a sufficient number of moments of good theater, such as the near-arrest scene, to reveal Wilde's potential gifts. Even his diction, if we ignore the frequent excesses, is often quite effective. The most striking anticipation of the later comedies is the presence of the Wildean dandy in the person of Prince Paul Maraloffski. Witty, urbane, languid, and devoted to the cultivation of the pleasures of life, Prince Paul is a striking forerunner of Lords Darlington, Illingworth, and Goring as the passage below reveals:

> Prince Petrovitch: I am bored with life, Prince. Since
> the opera season ended I have been a perpetual
> martyr to *ennui*.

> Prince Paul: The *maladie du siècle!* You want a new excite-
> ment, Prince. Let me see—you have been married twice
> already; suppose you try—falling in love for once.
> Baron Raff: I cannot understand your nature.
> Prince Paul (smiling): If my nature had been made to suit
> your comprehension rather than my own requirements,
> I am afraid I would have made a very poor figure in
> the world.
> Count Rouvaloff: There seems to be nothing in life about
> which you would not jest.
> Prince Paul: Ah! my dear Count, life is much too important
> a thing ever to talk seriously about it. (*Vera*, pp. 664-665)

This passage might easily fit into any one of the society comedies. In fact, Wilde liked Prince Paul's comment on the seriousness of life so much that he used it again in the first act of *Lady Windermere's Fan*.

II   The Duchess of Padua

The Duchess of Padua, Wilde's second play, was probably begun in 1882 during his tour of the United States. Wilde had accepted a thousand dollar advance from Mary Anderson, the American actress, for a "first class Five act tragedy to be completed on or before March 1st 1883"[7] and was entitled to another four thousand dollars upon acceptance of the play. While in Paris, where he went in order to finish the play before his deadline, he told Coquelin, the French actor, that his play consisted entirely of style: "Between them, Hugo and Shakespeare have exhausted every subject. Originality is no longer possible, even in sin. So there are no real emotions left—only extraordinary adjectives."[8] Nevertheless, Wilde finished his play in March and immediately sent it to Mary Anderson. Wilde learned soon after that the play had been refused. Mary Anderson cannot be faulted for rejecting it. Even Wilde at the end of his life admitted to Robert Ross that "*The Duchess* is unfit for publication—the only one of my works that comes under that category. But there are some good lines in it" (*Letters*, p. 757).

The plot of *The Duchess of Padua* focuses mainly upon young Guido Ferranti, who, after learning the secret of his birth from a mysterious Count Moranzone, swears to revenge the cruel murder of his father at the hands of the heartless Duke of Padua. At the instigation of Moranzone, Guido enters the Duke's service to gain his confidence, restraining his impulse to revenge until he receives a dagger from Moranzone. Guido and Beatrice, the Duchess, fall in love. On the occasion that Beatrice and Guido confess their love for each other, a package containing the prearranged signal arrives. Later that night, at the point of killing the Duke, Guido realizes that the murder will not only forever separate him from Beatrice but that such an act is unworthy of the memory of his father. Later Guido learns that Beatrice has killed the Duke for the sake of their love. When he spurns her, she orders him seized for the murder of the Duke. In the Court of Justice Guido at first refuses to admit or deny anything, but over the now-vindictive Duchess' objections he is allowed to speak. When Guido confesses that it was he who killed the Duke, the Duchess cries out his name as he is taken away. Later the heartbroken Beatrice brings the sleeping prisoner a ring and cloak with which to escape. While Guido sleeps she reveals her plan to drink poison and die in his place. After Beatrice dies in his arms, Guido plunges her dagger into his heart and falls dead across her body. When the Lord Justice enters, he draws the black cloak from the Duchess, "whose face is now the marble image of peace, the sign of God's forgiveness."

In *The Duchess of Padua* Wilde attempted a drama based on seventeenth-century tragic models. Present are the conventions of the revenge motif, Renaissance villainy, and even courtly love. All of these elements are fused into a melodrama of substantial, if misdirected, intensity. It is a play of violent peripeties, such as Guido's sudden decision in the third act not to murder the Duke because his father would not have approved of his revenge, or such unaccountable double reversals as Guido's sudden revulsion at the Duchess' commission of the murder that only moments before he himself had intended to commit. The closing scene in which Guido kills himself upon awakening to discover that the Duchess has taken her own life is a too obvious borrowing from Shakespeare's *Romeo and Juliet*. Nevertheless, such unlikely turns of plot and unfortunate borrowings are partly redeemed by Wilde's grasp of what makes for good theater.

III   Salome

Wilde wrote his poetic near-masterpiece in French during the autumn of 1891. According to Pearson, over lunch one day Oscar told the story in detail to a group of French writers. When he returned to his apartment, he noticed a blank book lying upon a table whereupon he began to write out his play. He wrote steadily until ten or eleven at night. Finding himself in need of some nourishment, he interrupted his composition and went to a nearby café. He asked the orchestra leader to play music in harmony with a play he was writing about "a woman dancing with her bare feet in the blood of a man she has craved for and slain." The orchestra leader played such strange and terrifying music that all conversation in the restaurant ceased and the listeners "looked at each other with blanched faces."[9] Although we cannot be certain of the truth of Wilde's story, it is clear that *Salome* like *The Picture of Dorian Gray* occupied a special place in his regard. During a bout of bad weather at the seaside in 1893, Wilde wrote to Frances Forbes-Robertson that he was consoling himself "by reading *Salome*, that terrible coloured little tragedy I once in some strange mood wrote" (*Letters*, p. 333).

Although Wilde's play was written in 1891, the French version was not published until February of 1893, while the English translation by Lord Alfred Douglas, which Wilde did not like,[10] appeared exactly one year later. Early in 1891 he read it to Sarah Bernhardt at her request. When she decided to produce it in London, he was filled with enthusiastic ideas: "I should like everyone on stage to be in yellow. . . . A violet sky. . . . Certainly a violet sky . . . and then in place of an orchestra, braziers of perfume. Think: the scented clouds rising and partly veiling the stage from time to time . . . a new perfume for each motion."[11] Rehearsals had gone on for three weeks when in June of 1892 the Lord Chamberlain refused to license the play on the ground that it presented Biblical characters. Wilde was furious and in a published interview deplored the tendency to deny to the stage the freedom granted to the other arts and insisted that "If the Censor refuses *Salome*, I shall leave England and settle in France where I will take out letters of naturalization. I will not be content to call myself a citizen of a country that shows such narrowness in its artistic judgment."[12]

In February of 1894 the English version was published in London. Aubrey Beardsley's highly sensual illustrations, with their phallic roses and candles, no doubt contributed to the general critical displeasure. *The Times* called it "an arrangement in blood and ferocity, morbid, *bizarre*, repulsive, and very offensive in its adaption of scriptural phraseology to situations the reverse of sacred. It is not ill-suited to some of the less attractive phases of Mme. Bernhardt's dramatic genius as it is vigorously written in some parts."[13]

Oscar replied that, although he was indifferent to *The Times*' opinion of the play, he wanted to point out that he did not write the play
for Sarah Bernhardt: "Such work is for the artisan in literature, not
for the artist" (*Letters*, p. 336). *The Pall Mall Gazette* accused Wilde
of borrowing too heavily from Théophile Gautier, Maurice Maeterlinck, and Gustave Flaubert.[14] William Archer, who was virtually
the only major critic to attack the decision to censor *Salome*, was
particularly impressed by the musical and pictorial qualities of the
drama:

> It is by methods borrowed from music that Mr. Wilde, without sacrificing
> its suppleness, imparts to his prose the firm texture, so to speak, of verse.
> Borrowed from music—may I conjecture?—through the intermediation of
> Maeterlinck. Certain it is that the brief melodious phrases, the chiming
> repetitions, the fugal effects beloved by the Belgian poet, are no less charac-
> teristic of Mr. Wilde's method. I am quite willing to believe, if necessary,
> that the two artists invented their similar devices independently, to meet a
> common need; but if, as a matter of fact, the one had taken a hint from the
> other, I do not see that his essential originality is thereby impaired. There is
> far more depth and body in Mr. Wilde's work than in Maeterlinck's. His
> characters are men and women, not filmy shapes of mist and moonshine.
> His properties, so to speak, are far more various and less conventional. His
> palette—I recur, in spite of myself, to the pictorial analogy—is infinitely
> richer. Maeterlinck paints in washes of water colour; Mr. Wilde attains the
> depth and brilliancy of oils.[15]

Archer demonstrates a keen contemporary insight into the poetic
qualities of Wilde's drama, and is evidently aware of the charges of
unwarranted borrowings from other writers.

Salome was first produced by Lugné-Poe on February 11, 1896, at
the Theatre de L'Oeuvre in Paris. The play was well received by
audience and critics. But Wilde never did see his play produced for
he was in prison in 1896 and the next production took place in 1902
at the Kleines Theatre in Berlin. The play was finally produced in
England on May 10 and 11, 1905. However, the greatest success
Wilde's drama was ever to have was as the libretto for Richard
Strauss' opera. Considering the nature of Wilde's drama and his
ideas concerning it, it is doubtful that he would have been dis-
pleased.

Wilde's dramatization of the story of Herodias' daughter dancing
before Herod for the head of John the Baptist is based upon the very

brief accounts in the sixth chapter of St. Mark and the fourteenth chapter of St. Matthew. Wilde, of course, alters the story significantly. In Wilde's version Salome rather than Herodias asks for the head of John the Baptist and accordingly suffers the fate meted out to her mother in the Scriptural account. Other likely sources are Victorien Sardou's *Theodora* (1884), Karl Huysman's *A Rebours* (1884) with its descriptions of Moreau's paintings, Gustav Flaubert's *Herodias* (1877), J. C. Heywood's dramatic poem "Salome" (1862), Théophile Gautier's *Une Nuit de Cleopatra* (1846), and Stephen Mallarmé's "Herodiade" (1869).[16] Wilde was also deeply influenced by the poetic imagery and repetitive patterns of the "Song of Solomon." This Biblical source is especially evident in Salome's long speeches praising Jokanaan's physical beauty. Wilde took such lines as "Thy lips are like a thread of scarlet" and "Thy neck is a tower of ivory" and combined them into "Thy mouth is like a band of scarlet on a tower of ivory."

A more subtle but important influence stems from the drama of Maurice Maeterlinck. Perhaps more than any other dramatist of his time Maeterlinck represents the effort in the closing decades of the nineteenth century to give substance to the ideals of a Symbolist drama. *Salome*, like the Symbolist plays of the Belgian writer, attempts to create a mood through carefully contrived nuances and repetitions. As in Maeterlinck's "static drama" the densely metaphoric language and the multiple parallelisms produce an intensification of mood that suited Wilde's purposes exactly. In a manner akin to Maeterlinck's, Wilde is attempting to create through language rather than action a sense of impending crisis and of the terrible and mysterious passions that destroy Salome. Wilde's one-act structure, like Maeterlinck's, contributes to such effects.

Although unity of tone seems to be what impresses us most powerfully in *Salome*, there is no plot beyond the expressed and implied remnants of the Biblical story. What little plot there is moves by a psychological rather than logical progression. This does not mean there is no structure. On the contrary, Jokanaan's voice speaking repeatedly from the cistern not only helps to unify the drama by providing indirect commentary upon the utterances and conditions of the main characters, but intensifies the sense of inevitable doom that permeates the drama. *Salome* is unified further by dramatic suspense. Salome's appearance is preceded by several lengthy descriptions of her strange beauty and actions. The long-delayed en-

trance of the beautiful Salome is paralleled by the later emergence
of Jokanaan from the cistern. The audience's anticipation of his appearance is heightened by a variety of questions by Salome about his
person. In similar fashion, Wilde intensifies our suspense and
curiosity concerning Salome's dance, her demand, and Herod's response. These and other devices give structure to the drama. But it
is the poetic substructure that Wilde creates that is the most important unifying element.

This unifying poetic substructure is comprised of parallelisms,
unusual associations, and patterns of imagery. For example, Wilde
creates an undercurrent of barely suppressed passion by the creation of insistent rhythms through the use of parallelism:

. . . Ah, Jokanaan, Jokanaan, thou wert the only man that I have loved. All
other men are hateful to me. But thou, thou wert beautiful! Thy body was a
column of ivory set on a silver socket. It was a garden full of doves and of
silver lilies. It was a tower of silver decked with shields of ivory. There was
nothing in the world so white as thy body. There was nothing in the world
so black as thy hair. In the whole world there was nothing so red as thy
mouth. (Salome, p. 574)

Wilde also subtly increases the rhythmic intensity of these parallelisms at the same time that he intensifies the contrast between the
beauty and the sensuality of the imagery until both reach a peak of
intensity at the close of the drama. A related poetic effect is derived
from the diversity and richness of Wilde's poetic associations. Wilde
often brings together images of the beautiful with the ugly, the
violent with the gentle, the intense with the subdued, the sensual
with the pure, and the cruel with the mild, as in the following:

Thy hair is horrible. It is covered with mire and dust. It is like a crown of
thorns which they have placed on thy forehead. It is like a knot of black
serpents writhing round thy neck. I love not thy hair . . . It is thy mouth
that I desire, Jokanaan. Thy mouth is like a band of scarlet on a tower of
ivory. It is like a pomegranate cut with a knife of ivory. The pomegranate-
flowers that blossom in the garden of Tyre, and are redder than roses, are
not so red. The red blast of trumpets, that herald the approach of kings, and
make afraid the enemy, are not so red. Thy mouth is redder than the feet of
those who tread the wine in the wine-press. Thy mouth is redder than the
feet of the doves who haunt the temples and are fed by the priests. It is
redder than the feet of him who cometh from a forest where he hath slain a
lion, and seen gilded tigers. Thy mouth is like a branch of coral that fishers

have found in the twilight of the sea, the coral that they keep for the kings. . . ! It is like the vermilion that the Moabites find in the mines of Moab, the vermilion that the kings take from them. It is like the bow of the King of the Persians, that is painted with vermilion, and is tipped with coral. There is nothing in the world so red as thy mouth. . . . Let me kiss thy mouth. (*Salome*, p. 559)

The effect of such associations is to suggest that psychological tensions and excitements of the characters and to impart an atmosphere of strangeness and even distance. Those moods and feelings which Salome is experiencing are not knowable within the ordinary ranges of human experience. It is in his achievement of such effects that Wilde's drama most resembles that of Maeterlinck.

Wilde was not only speaking metaphorically when he referred to his *Salome* as a "beautiful, coloured, musical" thing. A study of the language of *Salome* reveals patterns of color imagery which produce a poetic substructure that powerfully reinforces the larger and more obvious elements of the drama. Three basic color patterns predominate: white or ivory or silver, red, and black. Images of whiteness are usually associated with Salome. Her feet are described as "white doves" her hands as "white butterflies." She is described as a silver flower or a "white rose in a mirror of silver." Jokanaan's body is described as a "column of ivory," of white "like the lilies of a field"; but the colors red, vermilion, coral, and scarlet are also used apart from images of blood, to describe Jokanaan. Jokanaan's mouth is "like a band of scarlet," "a branch of coral." His tongue is a "red snake darting poison" or a "red viper." On the other hand, Jokanaan's hair is like "clusters of black grapes." Jokanaan prophesies that the sun will become "black like sackcloth of hair." Salome is struck by the blackness of the cistern. Altogether there are at least forty images of white, silver, or ivory, seventeen references to black or blackness, and thirty-eight references to red, vermilion, or scarlet. The frequency of such color imagery is striking but the patterns of occurrence are more significant. These color "motifs" or "refrains," as Wilde termed these images of red, scarlet, vermilion and so forth, increase in frequency and intensity until the close of the drama just before and after Salome is brought the head of Jokanaan and thus parallel Salome's succumbing to her strange passion.

The ever-intensifying desire of Salome for Jokanaan, the source of much of the fascination of Wilde's drama, is much more than sexual. Though some critics have made efforts to explain it in Freudian or

other terms,[17] Wilde has in mind something that resembles the
mysterious symbolic element Pater saw in Leonardo's *La Gioconda*:
"All the thoughts and experience of the world have etched and
molded there, in that which they have of power to refine and make
expressive the outward form, the animalism of Greece, the Lust of
Rome, the mysticism of the middle ages with its spiritual ambition
and imaginative loves, the return of the Pagan's world, the sins of
the Borgias. She is older than the rocks among which she sits; like
the vampire, she has been dead many times, and learned the secrets
of the grave" ("Leonardo da Vinci," *The Renaissance*). Huysman's
protagonist in *A Rebours*, a book known to have deeply influenced
Wilde's *Picture of Dorian Gray* as well as *Salome*, responds to Gustav Moreau's paintings of the legendary Salome in mystical as well as
sexual terms:

Des Esseintes saw realized at last the Salome, weird and superhuman, he
had dreamed of. No longer was she merely the dancing girl who extorts a
cry of lust and concupiscence from an old man by the lascivious contortions
of her body; who breaks the will, masters the mind of a King by the specta-
cle of her quivering bosoms, heaving belly and tossing thighs; she was now
revealed in a sense as the symbolic incarnation of world-old Vice, the goddess of immortal Hysteria, the Curse of Beauty supreme above all other
beauties by the cataleptic spasm that stirs her flesh and steels her
muscles,—a monstrous Beast of the Apocalypse, indifferent, irresponsible,
insensible, poisoning, like Helen of Troy of the old Classic fables, all who
come near her, all who see her, all who touch her.[18]

Wilde seems to be trying to create from the Salome legend the kind
of symbolic figure that Pater saw in Leonardo's *La Giaconda* and
Huysman saw in *Salome*. Such responses suggest a far more meaningful figure than most critics in the past have realized. San Juan
suggests that Wilde, by emphasizing the historical circumstances of
the events, evokes a powerful sense of historical crisis and change
that surrounds the drama. Thus, according to San Juan, "One can
make a persuasive argument that *Salome* is an allegory of a Spengle-
rian moment in European history."[19]

  The drama upon which Wilde lavished so much poetic attention is
indeed, as he termed it, a "terrible coloured little tragedy" (*Letters*,
p. 333). The conflicts with which Wilde struggled throughout his
career appear to be embodied in its symbolism. As Richard Ellmann
notes: "In *Salome* . . . the formulation is close to *Dorian Gray*, with

both opposites executed. Behind the figure of Jokanaan lurks the image of that perversely untouching, untouchable prophet John whom Wilde knew at Oxford." Although Ellman maintains that Jokanaan is not Ruskin, he is Ruskinism as Wilde understood that aspect of his own character. Thus, when Salome "evinces her appetite for strange experiences, her eagerness to kiss a totally disembodied lover in a relation at once totally sensual and totally 'mystical' (Wilde's own term for her), she shows something of that diseased contemplation for which Wilde had reprehended Pater."[20] The character of Jokanaan, then, represents Ruskinism or the demands of the moral, ethical life, for Wilde was attracted by the demands of Ruskin's moral earnestness, his call for a higher spiritual life. The character of Salome, on the other hand, represents the Paterian insistence upon cultivation of beauty and sensation and the desire for ever further ranges of experience. The linking of the imagery of whiteness with Jokanaan and redness with Salome and her intensifying desire reinforces this idea. The figure of Herod is readily seen as that of Wilde himself whose life and other dramas amply demonstrate the contrary impulses toward both principles. It is no secret that Herod in the story of John the Baptist plays much the same role as Pilate in the story of Christ. In the development of Wilde's other dramas we can see much the same struggle to find some sort of resolution between these two opposing principles. What begins in *Lady Windermere's Fan* as a conflict between the dandiacal devotion to beauty and sensation and the Philistine concern for what is moral and pure seemingly resolves itself in *The Importance of Being Earnest*.

IV   La Sainte Courtisane

In terms of technique *La Sainte Courtisane or The Woman Covered with Jewels*, which Wilde began in 1893 but never completed, represents his effort to write a drama by creating another world of the Biblical exotic that he realized so successfully in *Salome*. Wilde utilizes two minor figures, much like the Young Syrian and the Page of Herodias in *Salome*, as expository and descriptive devices. Similarly, a certain degree of dramatic suspense is produced by Myrrhina's prolonged questions concerning the hermit Honorius. The courtesan, like Salome, tempts the holy man; but, unlike Jokanaan, the young hermit Honorius is converted to a life of pleasure while the courtesan becomes a seeker after holiness. Wilde also creates, though with less success, a poetic language that closely resembles that of *Salome*. He employs the same highly embellished rhythmic style with its familiar parallelism, images of color, contrasts, and lengthy catalogues.

More interesting, however, to the student of Wilde's drama is the reappearance in this poetic drama of characters resembling the two central figures in *Salome*—Myrrhina, the worldly voluptuary, who with a terrible intensity seeks to satisfy her desires, and Honorius, the beautiful and holy ascetic, who affirms a life of denial leading to spiritual fulfillment. The transposition of their roles, by an internal process that the fragmentary nature of the drama makes unclear, suggests the same ambivalences that *Salome* more fully expresses.

V   A Florentine Tragedy

Only a fragment of *A Florentine Tragedy*, Wilde's blank verse tragedy, survives. Written about 1895, it represents another effort by Oscar Wilde to create poetic drama (*Letters*, p. 638). Rewritten to some extent after Wilde's release from prison, its chief interest for readers today lies in its relationship to the other poetic dramas and what it suggests about Wilde's potential development as a dramatist. As Roditi suggests, the play represents a kind of hybridization of the verse and setting of *The Duchess of Padua* and the one-act unity of Wilde's exotic *Salome*.[21] Wilde's blank verse possesses much of the intense emotional coloring, rhythmic patterns, and exotic richness of the language of *Salome*.

VI   Lady Windermere's Fan

Oscar Wilde's first comedy, *Lady Windermere's Fan*, gave the author some difficulty in composition. He wrote in 1891, "I am not satisfied with myself or my work. I can't get a grip of the play yet: I can't get my people real" (*Letters*, p. 282). Further difficulties arose during rehearsals. Wilde's concern for maintaining dramatic suspense conflicted sharply with that of the actors. Nevertheless, *Lady Windermere's Fan* was first produced at the St. James Theatre on February 20, 1892, with great success. With George Alexander as "Lord Windermere" and Marion Terry as "Mrs. Erlynne" Wilde's play represented the first genuinely brilliant comedy written in England since Sheridan's *School for Scandal*. But critical reactions to *Lady Windermere's Fan* were only grudgingly favorable. Wilde might have received more critical praise if he had not addressed his opening night audience with a cigarette in his hand. Although the audience enjoyed Wilde's speech and was appropriately mystified by seeing Wilde and some of his friends wearing green carnations, the critics seemed more offended by Wilde's cigarette than his congratulating the audience on a great performance. As the *Illustrated London News* growled, "The society that allows boys to puff cigarette-smoke into the faces of ladies in the theatre-corridors will condone the originality of a smoking author on the stage."[22] The best assessment is A. B. Walkley's in *The Speaker:* "It is no use telling me of the constructive faults, the flimsy plot, the unreasonable conduct of the characters. My answer is, 'I know all that; but the great thing is, that the play never bores me; and when a dramatist gives me such a perpetual flow of brilliant talk as Mr. Wilde gives, I am willing to forgive him all the sins in the dramatic Decalogue, and the rest.' "[23]

Wilde's first comedy concerns Lady Windermere, who learns from a gossipy Duchess that her husband has been visiting and giving large sums of money to a Mrs. Erlynne, a charming woman with a past. She confronts her husband, who alone knows that Mrs. Erlynne is the disgraced mother of Lady Windermere, with the evidence of his bankbook, but he denies any involvement. When he asks his wife to help Mrs. Erlynne reenter society, she coldly refuses and threatens to strike Mrs. Erlynne across the face with the fan she has just that day received from him as a birthday gift. In spite of her threat, he invites Mrs. Erlynne to the party. When the elegant Mrs. Erlynne arrives, Lady Windermere drops her fan and bows coldly. Later, when she overhears Mrs. Erlynne tell her husband that she will expect a two-thousand-pound settlement, she writes a note to her husband telling of her intention to run away with Lord Darlington, a notorious dandy. Mrs. Erlynne intercepts the note and later, in Lord Darlington's rooms, attempts to persuade the skeptical Lady Windermere not to ruin her life. When the men arrive, Mrs. Erlynne hides Lady Windermere behind a curtain and leaves the room. When Lord Windermere angrily demands that Darlington explain the presence of his wife's fan, Mrs. Erlynne enters and explains that she mistook the fan for her own. The next day Lord Windermere tells his wife that she will never be troubled by Mrs. Erlynne again, but Lady Windermere replies that she no longer thinks of her as a bad woman and that women ought not to be divided into the good and the bad. Mrs. Erlynne enters to return the fan and announce that she is soon to be married and will be living on the Continent.

Lady Windermere's Fan is built along four centers of conflict. We are introduced to the Lady Windermere–Lord Darlington and the Lady Windermere–Lord Windermere conflicts in the opening act. The two others, the Mrs. Erlynne–Lady Windermere and the Mrs. Erlynne–Lord Windermere conflicts are encountered in the second act. To this complexity Wilde introduced such well-worn dramatic clichés as the issue of "true identity" and the devices of the "long lost child," "the overheard conversation," the "discovered letter," the "concealment behind the curtain," and the "encounter with the other woman." However, Wilde cleverly alters several of these conventional patterns. For example, the true identities are never revealed, the "long-lost child" is really a long-lost parent, and the "encounter with the other woman" never really takes place. All these devices create suspense, but Wilde often fails to fulfill his audience's expectations.

Lady Windermere's adherence to an intolerant puritanical moral code is the central issue around which the play is organized. Because of her rigidity, she is incapable of understanding her husband's interest in Mrs. Erlynne's social success and, consequently, almost repeats the same social and moral error. By the end of the play, however, Lady Windermere is capable of arguing to her husband that "I don't think now that people can be divided into the good and the bad as though they were two separate races or creations" (*Lady Windermere's Fan*, p. 421). Although this issue is central to the drama, the dramatic actions hinge upon Mrs. Erlynne's saving her daughter from a moral chasm any Wildean Philistine would recognize.

Nevertheless, Wilde is really not interested in Lady Windermere or, to a lesser extent, Lord Windermere as characters; they function as puppets around which the characters in whom Wilde is really interested move. Lord Darlington, for example, is an incomplete rendering of the Wildean dandy and as such Wilde gives him much attention early in the play. He is the first dandy to appear in Wilde's comedies and his character is shaped appropriately.[24] He is an aristocrat whose natural superiority of intellect and wit is used to shock the Philistines around him. He is an absolute individualist who revels in exquisite sensations. His code of life is based upon the substitution of aesthetic values for moral ones. Like most Wildean dandies, one of Lord Darlington's functions is to shock or bewilder the Philistines. When the Duchess of Berwick tells Darlington that he must not know her daughter for he is far too wicked, he replies: "Don't say that, Duchess. As a wicked man I am a complete failure. Why, there are lots of people who say I have never really done anything wrong in the whole course of my life. Of course they only say it behind my back" (*Lady Windermere's Fan*, p. 389). On another occasion, after a discussion of marriage, Darlington succeeds in both shocking and bewildering the Duchess of Berwick:

Duchess of Berwick:	Dear Lord Darlington, how thoroughly depraved you are!
Lady Windermere:	Lord Darlington is trivial.
Lord Darlington:	Ah, don't say that, Lady Windermere.
Lady Windermere:	Why do you *talk* so trivially about life, then?
Lord Darlington:	Because I think that life is far too important a thing ever to talk seriously about it.
Duchess of Berwick:	What does he mean? Do, as a concession to my poor wits, Lord Darlington, just explain to me what you really mean.
Lord Darlington:	I think I had better not, Duchess. Nowadays to be intelligible is to be found out.

(Lady Windermere's Fan, p. 390)

We should note here that Wilde's use of the word "trivial" in the play must be understood for what it is. To Lord Darlington, the dandy, to be "trivial" would be to talk seriously about moral issues, while a concern for artificiality, beauty, and one's sensations, in other words what the Philistines would term "trivial" matters, are the truly serious concerns of life. But Lord Darlington's role as a dandy seems to diminish after the first act. He becomes little more than one side of a conventional love triangle and his dandiacal qualities correspondingly diminish. His insouciant wit cannot survive the deep commitments of passionate love, and he is eventually given such lines as "She is a good woman. She is the only good woman I have ever met in my life." Cecil Graham, who assumes the dandiacal role in the third act, replies to this sentiment as any good

dandy should: "Well, you are a lucky fellow! Why, I have met
hundreds of good women. I never seem to meet any but good
women. The world is perfectly packed with good women. To know
them is a middle-class education" (*Lady Windermere's Fan*, p. 417).
After this Wilde gives Darlington about a dozen more lines and
excludes him entirely from the last act.

Wilde never loses interest in Mrs. Erlynne, however. It is no
wonder, for not only is she the wicked woman with a past, but on
occasion she functions in the dandiacal role and gets the witty lines.
When Windermere recoils with horror at Mrs. Erlynne's lack of
repentance, she replies:

I suppose, Windermere, you would like me to retire into a convent, or
become a hospital nurse, or something of that kind, as people do in silly
modern novels. That is stupid of you, Arthur; in real life we don't do such
things—not as long as we have any good looks left, at any rate. No—what
consoles one nowadays is not repentance, but pleasure. Repentance is quite
out of date. And besides, if a woman really repents, she has to go to a bad
dressmaker, otherwise no one believes in her. And nothing in the world
would induce me to do that. (*Lady Windermere's Fan*, p. 425)

A little earlier she tells Windermere that she intends to leave England because "London is too full of fogs and—and serious people."
A few lines later, when Windermere reproaches her for intruding
in his home after being discovered in Darlington's apartments, she
replies "My dear Windermere, manners before morals!" (*Lady
Windermere's Fan*, pp. 422-423).

Wilde's character is forced by the exigencies of plot to play a
double role. She is the supposed temptress of Windermere and the
fallen woman of the world who has "no ambition to play the part of
the mother." She is also a Wildean commentator who must also
function as the devoted mother to her unsuspecting daughter, a
mother who at the finding of her daughter's fatal letter cries, "What
can I do? I feel a passion awakening within me that I never felt
before. What can it mean? The daughter must not be like the
mother—that would be terrible. How can I save her?" (*Lady Windermere's Fan*, p. 409). She is appealing in this speech and others to
those moral values she supposedly discards by the end of the play.
Otherwise her speech becomes not a personal confession but an
expedient means of persuasion. The difficulty, as Ian Gregor points

out, is that "Wilde presents her alternately as both 'inside' and 'outside' the action of the play—a protagonist in a moral plot turning, at times, into a Wildean commentator."[25]

The direction of Wilde's irony can be grasped when we realize the characters' state of enlightenment at the end of the drama. Lady Windermere has accepted Mrs. Erlynne's advice not to reveal their secret to Lord Windermere and is willing to relax her moral rigidity. Lord Windermere will continue to conceal Mrs. Erlynne's real identity from Lady Windermere. In addition, neither Lady Windermere nor her husband's judgments of Mrs. Erlynne are accurate. Mrs. Erlynne's husband-to-be, who says that she has "explained every demmed thing," has in reality been told nothing. The artificiality of the final circumstances of the drama combined with the artistic manipulation of almost everyone by Mrs. Erlynne in order to fulfill her designs, is the substance of Wilde's major point. Just as Wilde's final revelation in "The Decay of Lying" is "that Lying, the telling of beautiful untrue things, is the proper aim of Art" ("Decay of Lying," p. 320), so Mrs. Erlynne has fashioned a beautiful false image of herself. She embodies, albeit in incomplete form, the Wildean theory of personality, that creating a work of art out of one's life is the highest artistic achievement. This idea is developed incompletely, but a failure to recognize it weakens our understanding of plot and character and reduces Darlington, Cecil Graham, and Mrs. Erlynne's epigrammatic lines to witty excrescences.

In this, the first of his society comedies, Wilde, like Ibsen and Shaw, is rebelling aginst the Philistinism of the age. Unlike Shaw and Ibsen, however, his plot embodies a moral rightness sufficient to warm the heart of any Victorian censor. Morse Peckham argues convincingly that although Lady Windermere discovers that she is capable of evil she never questions the standard by which she judges herself and others. While Mrs. Erlynne argues that "Ideals are dangerous things. Realities are better. They wound, but they are better" (*Lady Windermere's Fan*, p. 427), Lady Windermere replies "If I lost my ideals, I should lose everything." There is no question, as Peckham argues, that Wilde is attacking "the inadequacy of the traditional categories of good and evil."[26] But Lady Windermere does not have, as Mrs. Erlynne points out, "the kind of brains that enables a woman to get back. . . . neither the wit nor the courage" (*Lady Windermere's Fan*, p. 413). Wilde seems not to be arguing, using a very ordinary Lady Windermere as a case in point, the improbability of a Philistine middle class reforming itself. He has already, and however contradictorily, made his central point through the commentaries of Lord Darlington, Cecil Graham, and Mrs. Erlynne. When she urges her husband to take her to the Rose Garden at Shelby, where "the roses are white and red," Wilde is reiterating Lady Windermere's recent recognition that in the same old world "good and evil, sin and innocence, go through it hand and hand" (*Lady Windermere's Fan*, p. 429). Like the beautiful fragile ladies in the paintings of Wilde's favorite artists, Francois Boucher, Jean Honoré Fragonard, Antoine Watteau, Lady Windermere now sees her existence in terms of beauty, not rigid morality. Even Lady Windermere is allowed a touch of the dandy.

VII   A Woman of No Importance

A Woman of No Importance, originally entitled *Mrs. Arbuthnot*, was apparently completed in late February of 1893 at Babbacombe Cliff, Torquay, a house with "Rosetti drawings, and a window by Burne-Jones, and many lovely things and colours" (*Letters*, p. 335). As in his earlier comedy Wilde drew from the vicinity the names of several of his characters. Hunstanton and Illingworth, for example, were derived from places in the vicinity of Cromer. For his basic plot Wilde drew mainly upon Dumas' *Le Fils naturel*, a play about a young working girl who has been seduced by a young aristocrat who refuses to marry her. Her son develops into a young man of splendid character who eventually rejects his father's offer to legitimize his birth.

A Woman of No Importance first appeared at the Haymarket Theatre on April 19, 1893, and was received enthusiastically. Critical reactions to Wilde's new play were favorable although critics complained that Wilde's dramas lacked action. Wilde's reply was characteristic: "I wrote the first act of *A Woman of No Importance* in answer to the critics who said that *Lady Windermere's Fan* lacked action. In the act in question there was absolutely no action. It was a perfect act."[27]

The basic conflict of Wilde's second comedy is found in the struggle between Lord Illingworth, a charming aristocrat of wicked reputation, and Mrs. Arbuthnot, a woman who early in her life had trusted a man and been disgraced, for possession of their illegitimate son, Gerald Arbuthnot. Because the secret of his birth has been Mrs. Arbuthnot's alone, she cannot explain to her son why she objects to his taking a position as secretary to Lord Illingworth, who has deeply influenced Gerald with his dandiacal life and ideals. Eventually Lord Illingworth reveals his true nature by insulting Hester Worsley, a rich and rather puritanical American girl who is in love with Gerald and believes that all men and women who sin should be banished from the society of good people. Gerald vows to kill Lord Illingworth; and, consequently, his mother is forced to reveal that Lord Illingworth is his father. Gerald takes the conventional Philistine attitude and insists that Lord Illingworth marry his mother. Mrs. Arbuthnot insists that this would be an even greater disgrace. When Hester supports her, Gerald is finally convinced of the rightness of his mother's position. Lord Illingworth, who had contemptuously referred to Mrs. Arbuthnot earlier as "a woman of no importance," is dismissed in similar terms at the close of the drama.

The immediate impression that *A Woman of No Importance* provides is that Wilde has gone to great lengths to embellish his drama with even greater quantities of the clever talk that distinguished his earlier comedy. In fact, *A Woman of No Importance* abounds in brilliant wit and dandified characters. Lord Illingworth, Wilde's chief spokesman and the figure who epitomizes the elegant and artificial world to which Gerald Arbuthnot aspires, is surrounded by many only slightly less brilliant satellites. Lady Caroline, Lady Hunstanton, Lady Stutfield, and especially Lady Allonby are dandies who represent, no less than Lord Illingworth, the insiders of the societal norm in Wilde's comedy. Wilde puts epigram after epigram into the mouths of these characters. Wilde rarely equaled the brilliance of the exchange between Mrs. Allonby and Lord Illingworth at the close of the first act:

Lord Illingworth:	Shall we go in to tea?
Mrs. Allonby:	Do you like such simple pleasures?
Lord Illingworth:	I adore simple pleasures. They are the last refuge of the complex. But, if you wish, let us stay here. Yes, let us stay here. The Book of Life begins with a man and a woman in a garden.
Mrs. Allonby:	It ends with Revelations.

Lord Illingworth:	You fence divinely. But the button has come off your foil.
Mrs. Allonby:	I have still the mask.
Lord Illingworth:	It makes your eyes lovelier.

(*A Woman of No Importance*, p. 443)

So concerned is Wilde with strengthening this element in his second drama that he does not hesitate to rework or simply borrow lines from his other works.

Wilde utilizes the same opposing sets of values he employed in *Lady Windermere's Fan*. In the earlier play the dandy and his values are set against conventional society. In the second comedy, however, the conflict between these two opposing sets of values is heightened and a particularly significant social realignment has taken place. The dandiacal society represented by Lord Illingworth, Mrs. Allonby, and others is presented as the dominant one, whereas the Philistine or "conventional" society, as represented by Mrs. Arbuthnot and Hester Worsley, is placed outside of the social mainstream. This conflict between the opposing dandiacal and Philistine points of view, an opposition present in most of Wilde's work, enables Wilde not only to exercise his wit but to illuminate his ideas. For example, the witty conversation between Lord Illingworth and Gerald at the opening of the third act is clearly derived from the conversation between Lord Henry Wotton and Dorian in the second chapter of *The Picture of Dorian Gray*. Just as Lord Henry attempts to seduce the innocent Dorian to a New Hedonism, Lord Illingworth attempts to convert Gerald to modern dandyism:

Lord Illingworth:	I suppose your mother is very religious, and that sort of thing.
Gerald:	Oh, yes, she's always going to church.
Lord Illingworth:	Ah! She is not modern, and to be modern is the only thing worth being nowadays. You want to be modern, don't you, Gerald? You want to know life as it really is. Not to be put off with any old-fashioned theories about life. Well, what you have to do at present is simply to fit yourself for the best society. A man who can dominate a London dinner-table can

> dominate the world. The future belongs to the
> dandy. It is the exquisites who are going to rule.
> (*A Woman of No Importance*, p. 459)

A moment later Wilde provides occasion for Gerald to ask no fewer than twelve successive questions, each of which provides Lord Illingworth with dramatic opportunity to expound his dandiacal creed.

The Philistine element is, in parallel fashion, more strongly embodied in the dramatic elements of *A Woman of No Importance* than in any of Wilde's other comedies. Two characters, Mrs. Arbuthnot, the abandoned unwed mother of Gerald, and Hester Worsley, the "Puritan" from America, serve as spokeswomen for the moralist position. Early in the play, Wilde casts Hester in the familiar Wildean role of the unyielding moralist. Hester's moral stance is so harsh and unyielding that an audience finds little with which to sympathize. For those women who have been victimized by predatory dandies such as Lord Henry Weston, Hester has no sympathy, only ostracization: "Lord Henry Weston! I remember him, Lady Hunstanton. A man with a hideous smile and a hideous past. He is asked everywhere. No dinner-party is complete without him. What of those whose ruin is due to him? They are outcasts. They are nameless. If you met them in the street you would turn your head away. I don't complain of their punishment. Let all women who have sinned be punished" (*A Woman of No Importance*, p. 449). But her harshness is not reserved for women alone, for a few lines later Hester insists that "till you count what is a shame in a woman to be infamy in a man, you will always be unjust. . . ." Wilde follows Hester's passionate attack upon the double standard with Lady Caroline's insultingly trivial request: "Might I, dear Miss Worsley, as you are standing up, ask you for my cotton that is just behind you? Thank you." Hester's rejection of the dandiacal compliments of Lord Henry Weston—the man without whom, like Lord Henry Wotton, no dinner party is complete—is similarly undercut by Lady Caroline's insistence that in spite of Lord Henry's infamy "He is excellent company, and has one of the best cooks in London, and after a good dinner one can forgive anybody, even one's own relations" (*A Woman of No Importance*, p. 450). The effect is to undercut the possibility of the audience, at this point, taking Hester's plea

seriously. Thus, with Wilde's help, the moralist is vanquished by
the dandy.

The audience's response to the harshness of Hester's Puritan
code, as Wilde no doubt intends, must be negative; yet Hester's
implied attack upon the injustice of a double standard must as-
suredly gain at least partial acceptance. Moreover, Hester's opin-
ions certainly represent Wilde's marital views, just as the following
condemnation of English society by Hester is expressive of Wilde's
social views: "Living, as you all do, on others and by them, you
sneer at self-sacrifice, and if you throw bread to the poor, it is
merely to keep them quiet for a season. With all your pomp and
wealth and art you don't know how to live—you don't even know
that. You love the beauty that you can see and touch and handle, the
beauty that you can destroy, and do destroy, but of the unseen
beauty of life, of the unseen beauty of a higher life, you know
nothing" (*A Woman of No Importance*, p. 449). Hester's attack expresses the same frustrations with English life that Wilde's "The
Soul of Man Under Socialism" does and, in fact, suggests several of
its salient ideas, especially Wilde's denunciation of an English society which, in its hostility and indifference to the arts, places obsta-
cles in the path of man's evolution towards individualism. Wilde,
apparently unmindful of the larger purposes of his drama, is more
concerned here and elsewhere with the substantial amount of
dramatic irony Hester's unyielding attitude makes possible than he
is with the dramatic problem stemming form his undercutting of
characters who serve not only as his partial spokeswomen but ultimate heroines.

On the whole, Wilde's second comedy appears to be a conscious
attempt to create another success by reworking and intensifying the
basic conflict of *Lady Windermere's Fan*, thus enabling the
dramatist to give greater emphasis to the element which lay at the
roots of his first dramatic success—namely, his wit. However, the
inevitable effect of Wilde's intensification of this basic conflict is to
màke a convincing resolution of the issues more difficult. Paradoxi-
cally, *A Woman of No Importance* is the least successful of Wilde's
comedies, yet nearly the wittiest. Wilde, apparently, needed to
learn his limitations. He lacked the imaginative sympathy or was
unwilling to exercise it, requisite to effective handling of what we
have termed the Philistine element of his plots. In addition, he
needed to free the dandiacal element, his area of greatest strength,

from any conflict with his larger dramatic purposes. He achieved this by mitigating his attacks upon the middle class and concentrating upon the form of his dramas.

VIII   An Ideal Husband

An Ideal Husband, according to Frank Harris, was based on a story that he had told Wilde about Disraeli's making money by entrusting the Rothschilds with the purchase of Suez Canal shares.[28] Pearson discounts the significance of Harris' claim by arguing that "Sardou must have suggested it to Harris, as it is to be found in that playwright's *Dora*."[29] *An Ideal Husband* was first performed at the Theater Royal, Haymarket, on January 3, 1895, with great success. Henry James, whose own play *Guy Domville* also opened the same night, saw Wilde's play at its opening. He felt the play was "so helpless, so crude, so bad, so clumsy, feeble, and vulgar" that he wondered "How *can* my piece do anything with a public with whom *that* is a success?"[30] James was at least partly right, for his own play closed February 2 to make room for the *The Importance of Being Earnest*.

Wilde's third comedy, *An Ideal Husband*, presents in Lady Chiltern another Puritan who cannot forgive anyone who has ever done a wicked or shameful deed. Her husband Robert, whom she idealizes, has long ago made his fortune by dishonorably selling a government secret. Mrs. Cheveley, a dishonest former school acquaintance of Lady Chiltern, attempts to blackmail Sir Robert into supporting a fraudulent Argentine canal project. Sir Robert is certain he will lose his wife if his secret is revealed, but Lord Goring, the Wildean dandy, encourages him to fight Mrs. Cheveley. When Lady Chiltern learns of her husband's past, she castigates him and rejects his pleas for forgiveness. Later, Lord Goring receives a seemingly compromising letter from Lady Chiltern. By confronting Mrs. Cheveley with a diamond brooch she had stolen, Lord Goring obtains the damaging letter Sir Robert had written long ago that revealed his guilt, but Mrs. Cheveley obtains Lady Chiltern's letter and declares her intention to send it to Sir Robert that night. The next day Sir Robert officially denounces the fraudulent canal scheme and is reunited with his wife. The letter Mrs. Cheveley had sent had been an affectionate and forgiving one that had been intended for him all along. Lord Goring wins the lovely Mabel Chiltern while

Lady Chiltern discovers that "Nobody is incapable of doing a foolish thing. Nobody is incapable of doing a wrong thing."

Although Wilde's *An Ideal Husband*, like *Lady Windermere's Fan* and *A Woman of No Importance*, centers around a conflict caused by a wife or fiance's unyielding moral rigidity, the manner in which the dandy is related to this conflict is quite new. The dandy in Wilde's two earlier comedies was a dangerous though charming villain. Lord Darlington in *Lady Windermere's Fan* nearly succeeds in breaking up a marriage. Lord Illingworth in *A Woman of No Importance* is a betrayer of women. Both figures, however, function as spokesmen for the dandiacal way of life and, on occasion, as Wildean commentators.

When in the earlier plays these figures are discredited as the conventionally moral plots demanded, there is some question in the reader's mind about the concomitant condemnation of their dandiacal message. Such a divided reaction Wilde surely did not intend. More likely Wilde was attempting to write plays that would be appreciated and understood by both Philistine and cognoscente at two different levels. Lord Goring, however, in *An Ideal Husband* represents a significant development in Wilde's treatment of the dandy. Although he retains his role as dandy and Wildean commentator, he loses the usual role as villain. Mrs. Cheveley has assumed this function. Wilde retains the woman with the past, but in this case she sins more than she is sinned against. Another vestigial remainder of the villainous dandy can be discovered in Baron Arnheim. Although, we never meet him, we learn that he is an aesthete of exquisite tastes who early seduced Lord Chiltern to his doctrine of wealth. At the close of the play, when Sir Robert Chiltern is about to terminate his political career with his wife's misguided acquiescence, it is Lord Goring's long sermon on the roles of men and women which saves the day: "Women are not meant to judge us, but to forgive us when we need forgiveness. Pardon, not punishment, is their mission" (*An Ideal Husband*, p. 548). Wilde could hardly realize how unacceptable such role distinctions would be for us today, but he is clearly reflecting the views of the mass of Englishmen of his time. Thus, the dandy has lost his sting.

In *An Ideal Husband* Wilde realigns his characters in such a way that, for the first time, the villain (villainess in this case) is an antagonist of the dandy. Mrs. Cheveley, in spite of her role as heavy, is as much a dandy as Lord Goring. Mrs. Cheveley, who is "a work

of art, on the whole, but showing the influence of too many schools
(*An Ideal Husband*, p. 484), like Lord Goring, believes that life is a
pose:

Sir Robert Chiltern:	To attempt to classify you, Mrs. Cheveley, would be an impertinence. But may I ask, at heart, are you an optimist or a pessimist? Those seem to be the only two fashionable religions left to us nowadays.
Mrs. Cheveley:	Oh, I'm neither. Optimism begins in a broad grin, and Pessimism ends with blue spectacles. Besides, they are both of them merely poses.
Sir Robert Chiltern:	You prefer to be natural?
Mrs. Cheveley:	Sometimes. But it is such a very difficult pose to keep up.

(An Ideal Husband, pp. 486-487)

Mrs. Cheveley, who prefers books in "yellow covers," sees life as an
art form. In a conversation with Mrs. Markby, another dandy in a
play where the dandies outnumber the Philistines, she expounds
Wilde's view of life as an art form:

Mrs. Cheveley:	. . . Fathers have so much to learn from their sons nowadays.
Lady Markby:	Really, dear? What?
Mrs. Cheveley:	The art of living. The only really Fine Art we have produced in modern times.

(An Ideal Husband, pp. 531-532)

Such comments are echoed in the words of other Wildean dandies.
Mrs. Cheveley serves as spokeswoman on occasion for several Wildean ideas but Wilde insures that we see her as a villainess by
making her a thief, a blackmailer, and a protégé of the evil Baron
Arnheim. Moreover, her status as a dandy is further undercut by
her conception of human relations as commercial transactions. The
benevolent dandy must be above such sordidness.

A Wildean idea given especially strong emphasis in *An Ideal
Husband* is that life is as capable of artistic form and meaning as a
painting or a poem. The idea of life as an art form is not so explicitly
presented as it is in *Intentions* or *The Picture of Dorian Gray*; but

the emphasis on art, artists, artistic form, masks, poses, and such
suggests the deep importance of this idea. Some characters are com-
pared to works of art. Mrs. Cheveley is described as "a work of
art . . . but showing the influence of too many schools"; Mabel
Chiltern is really "like a Tanagra statuette"; Lord Caversham is "a
fine Whig type. Rather like a portrait by Laurence." Others are
revealed as potential subjects. Watteau would have loved to paint
Mrs. Marchmont and Lady Basildon, those "types of exquisite fragil-
ity." Anthony Vandyke would have liked to paint Sir Robert Chiltern's head. The opening scene takes place beneath a "large
eighteenth century French tapestry—representing the Triumph of
Love, from a design by Boucher—that is stretched on the staircase
wall." Sir Robert Chiltern is a collector of art objects and has a
particularly fine collection of Corots. Each of these artists, especially
Boucher and Watteau, throughout or at some stage of his career
represents a commitment to artificiality, sensuousity, and escapism.
Phipps, Lord Goring's butler, is described as a "mask with a manner," one who "represents the dominance of form." These details
reinforce the Wildean precept that the artistic form of one's life is
all-important. This notion was central to the dandiacal creed.

The imagery of masks which so permeates this drama not only
reinforces the life-as-art-form theme but buttresses the plot in several other ways. Events hinge upon reversals of conceptions of self
and others. Lady Chiltern cannot conceive of committing a serious
social error, nor can she imagine being married to a man of anything
but impeccable character. Both conceptions prove faulty. Sir Robert
presents a public mask of absolute personal integrity but has actually
built his fortune and career upon a deception. Lady Chiltern con-
demns her husband at one point for not preserving his mask of
integrity by lying to her. Sir Robert, at another point in the drama,
refuses Lord Goring's advice to confess because he believes his wife
"does not know what weakness or temptation is" (*An Ideal Husband*, p. 529). Ironically, neither of the two principals can see
beyond the mask of the other.

In this, the third of Wilde's society comedies, the moralistic plot
does not jar so sharply against the anti-Philistine and dandiacal elements. This harmony is achieved primarily by making Lord Goring
the ally of the principal characters in their struggle against the
wicked Mrs. Cheveley. The political satire also helps to dissipate
the discord that existed in the earlier comedies between the comic

themes and the serious ones. The plethora of rather hackneyed theatrical devices is evident as well as the insistence upon the melodramatic. More significant than all the above, however, is the substantial movement towards dramatic unity by the uniting of the Wildean life-as-art-form, "mask," "game," and "pose" themes with his central dramatic action. Wildean dandyism can be clearly recognized as a fundamental aspect of Wilde's thought and method and not a thematic excrescence. Imperfect as the blend may be, it illustrates Wilde's substantial growth as a dramatist and presages the perfection of Wilde's comedic form in *The Importance of Being Earnest*.

IV   The Importance of Being Earnest

The Importance of Being Earnest, Wilde's comic masterpiece, was written during the summer of 1894. Writing to Lord Alfred Douglas from Worthing near the seashore, he spoke of his pleasure at his progress: "I have been doing nothing here but bathing and playwriting. My play is really funny: I am quite delighted with it. But it is not shaped yet" (*Letters*, p. 362). Wilde writes that "the real charm of the play, if it is to have a charm, must be in the dialogue. The plot is slight . . . but . . . adequate" (*Letters*, p. 359). In general it was "the best I have ever written" (*Letters*, p. 369). The original, entitled *Lady Lancing*, was apparently finished in October of 1894. Wilde was anxious that George Alexander should play the part of John Worthing (*Letters*, p. 376). At Alexander's suggestion Wilde revised the play into three acts, a definite improvement on the four-act original. Commenting in his inimitable style upon the revisions, Wilde insisted that "the first act is ingenious, the second beautiful, the third abominably clever."[31]

The Importance of Being Earnest was produced in London at the St. James Theatre on the evening of February 14, 1895. Wilde's complete triumph was perhaps nowhere better expressed than in Hamilton Fyfe's opening night review for the *New York Times*: "Since *Charley's Aunt* was first brought from the provinces to London I have not heard such unrestrained, incessant laughter from all parts of the theatre, and those laughed the loudest whose approved mission it is to read Oscar long lectures in the press on his dramatic and ethical shortcomings."[32] The reviewers, with several exceptions, not only were delighted with the new play, but in many cases

assessed it in terms of Wilde's own artistic dicta. The questions
William Archer raises in his review seem remarkably Wildean:

> What can a poor critic do with a play which raises no principle, whether of
> art or morals, creates its own canons and conventions, and is nothing but an
> absolutely wilful expression of an irrepressibly witty personality? Mr. Pater,
> I think (or is it someone else?), has an essay on the tendency of all art to
> verge towards, and merge in, the absolute art—music. He might have
> found an example in *The Importance of Being Earnest*, which imitates
> nothing, represents nothing, is nothing, except a sort of *rondo capriccioso*,
> in which the artist's fingers run with crisp irresponsibility up and down the
> keyboard of life.[33]

Other critics recognized Wilde's single-minded devotion to pure
comic effect. A. B. Walkley, always one of Wilde's keenest critics,
termed Wilde an "artist in sheer nonsense," and noted that "There
has been good nonsense in his previous stage-work, but it failed to
give unalloyed pleasure, either because it adopted serious postures
or was out of harmony with an environment of seriousness."[34] But
not quite everyone was pleased. George Bernard Shaw, not surprisingly, was "unable to perceive any uncommon excellence in its
presentations." But Shaw admitted his bias: "unless comedy touches
me as well as amuses me, it leaves me with a sense of having wasted
my evening"[35]—a not unexpected reaction from the serious Shaw to
the first of Wilde's dramas to realize completely the principle for
which he had been striving in his three earlier comedies that "the
sphere of Art and the sphere of Ethics are absolutely distinct and
separate" ("Critic as Artist," p. 393).

The complex plot of Oscar Wilde's fourth comedy is filled with
such stock devices as intercepted letters, inopportune appearances,
mistaken identities, quid pro quos, peripeties, and secrets from the
past. Basically, the plot centers upon Algernon Moncrieff and Jack
Worthing. Jack wants to marry Gwendolen Fairfax but Algernon
refuses to give his permission to marry his cousin until Jack clears up
the question of Cecily. Jack pretends ignorance; but, when Algernon reads the inscription "From little Cecily with her fondest love
to Uncle Jack" on a cigarette case that Jack has misplaced, Jack
confesses that old Mr. Cardew, who adopted him when he was a
boy, had made him guardian of his granddaughter Miss Cecily Cardew. Jack admits that he has always pretended to have a wicked
younger brother named Earnest. Thus, he has always been known

as Uncle Jack to Cecily rather than Earnest, his real name. Algernon has in similar fashion invented an imaginary sick friend named Bunbury who provides him with an excuse to go out into the country whenever he chooses. Later, when Jack confesses his love for Gwendolen, she tells him that she can never love anyone whose name is not Earnest. However, Lady Bracknell refuses to recognize the engagement when Jack reveals that he was found in a handbag in Victoria Station.

When Algernon, masquerading later as Jack's brother Earnest, meets Cecily, she tells him that she can never love anyone named Algernon. Both men make arrangements with a Dr. Chausuble to have their names changed. When Cecily and Gwendolen finally meet, they discover the double deception and decide that neither of them is engaged to anyone. Both girls, however, decide to forgive Jack and Algernon when they learn of their proposed christenings. When Dr. Chausuble mentions the name of Cecily's tutor, Miss Prism, Lady Bracknell starts and insists that she be sent for. Miss Prism, who years before was a nurse in the family, appears and quails when Lady Bracknell demands "Where is that baby?" Prism explains that she left the baby in the perambulator with the manuscript of a novel she had written. She confesses that in a moment of abstraction she had deposited the manuscript in the bassinet and the baby in a large handbag. When Jack, who has been listening intently, asks her where she deposited the handbag, she replies that she left it in the cloakroom of Victoria Station. Jack rushes out in great excitement and returns clutching a handbag which Miss Prism identifies as hers. When Jack embraces her and calls her mother, she recoils in indignation. Lady Bracknell explains that Jack is the son of her sister Mrs. Moncrieff and, consequently, Algernon's elder brother. Jack then discovers that his real name is Earnest. Gwendolen is delighted. Miss Prism and Dr. Chausuble embrace, Algernon and Cecily embrace, and Jack and Gwendolen embrace, all exclaiming "At last!" When Lady Bracknell accuses him of displaying signs of triviality, Jack replies, "On the contrary, Aunt Augusta, I've now realised for the first time in my life the vital Importance of Being Earnest."

In *The Importance of Being Earnest* Wilde has finally created what his four previous dramas have suggested he would do. He has created a drama that is a perfect artistic expression of his artistic credo. Moreover, he has created a dramatic world built upon his aesthetic principles that actually works. To say it "comes to life" would be perhaps inaccurate and, no doubt, Wilde would object to the term. Although the characters are unreal, the plot impossible, the language artificial, and its ideas trivial, Wilde succeeds in setting into motion a brilliant, artificial, dramatic world. William Archer, it will be recalled, was pleased with Wilde's drama but was uncertain of how to criticize it, for it "imitates nothing, represents nothing, means nothing, is nothing, except a sort of *rondo capriccioso*, in which the artist's fingers run with crisp irresponsibility up and down the keyboard of life." Archer, like other contemporary reviewers, perceived the nature of the drama but missed its significance. But Wilde had explained it all quite neatly in his "Critic as Artist": "From time to time the world cries out against some charming artistic poet, because, to use its hackneyed and silly phrase, he has 'nothing to say.'" But if he had something to say, he would probably say it, and the result would be tedious. It is just because he has no new message, that he can do beautiful work. He gains his inspiration from form, and from form purely, as an artist should. A real passion would ruin him. Whatever actually occurs is spoiled for art" ("Critic as Artist," II, p. 398). Wilde's earlier dramas were marred by his efforts to devise plots which pitted dandiacal principles against Philistine. As Wilde himself should have known, when he attempted to depict a "real passion" in *A Woman of No Importance*, his drama was ruined. In *The Importance of Being Earnest*, however, such conflicts are gone. The dandies are neither villains nor saviors. They simply are everywhere. Wilde has brilliantly succeeded in creating a totally artificial world where form is the beginning and end of things.

At the very beginning of his comedy, Wilde suggests that artificial patterns or forms of behavior will be his central concern. Algernon asks Lane, his butler, whether he has heard his playing of the piano. Lane, the perfect dandiacal butler, replies in perfect form that he did not think it polite to listen. Algernon's subsequent reply reveals Wilde's central dramatic concern: "I'm sorry for that, for your sake. I don't play accurately—anyone can play accurately—but I play with wonderful expression. As far as the piano is concerned, sentiment is my forte. I keep science for Life" (*Earnest*, p. 321). A moment later, when Jack confesses his motives for being "Earnest in town and Jack in the country" and maintains that this is "the whole truth pure and simple," Algernon replies that "The truth is rarely pure and never

simple. Modern life would be very tedious if it were either, and
modern literature a complete impossibility!" (*Earnest*, p. 326).
From this point on, as Richard Foster reveals, "Wilde's play is to be
a satiric demonstration of how art can lie romantically about human
beings and distort the simple laws of real life with melodramatic
complications and improbably easy escapes from them."[36] Life is
important only in that it may provide a portion of the raw material
out of which we fashion art. In fact, without the "distortions" of Art,
life would be at best tedious. Only the Philistine allows himself to be
trapped within the conventions of everyday life.

Wilde, in order to reinforce this idea, bases much of the action
and language of the play upon inversions of stock romantic speech
and situations. The scene in which Jack learns that Gwendolen has
loved him from the moment Algernon first mentioned to her that he
had a friend called Earnest illustrates the technique:

Jack:	You really love me, Gwendolen?
Gwendolen:	Passionately!
Jack	Darling! You don't know how happy you've made me.
Gwendolen:	My own Earnest!
Jack:	But you don't really mean to say that you couldn't love me if my name wasn't Earnest?
Gwendolen:	But your name is Earnest.
Jack:	Yes, I know it is. But supposing it was something else? Do you mean to say you couldn't love me then?
Gwendolen (glibly):	Ah! that is clearly a metaphysical speculation, and like most metaphysical speculations has very little reference at all to the actual facts of real life, as we know them.

(*Earnest*, p. 330)

This scene is an inverted parody of the stock romantic situation in
which the lovers' devotion alone, not their names, has meaning.
There is no denying this passage is nonsense. But it is delightful,
artifical nonsense. At the close of the first act Algernon maintains
that he loves scrapes for "They are the only things that are never
serious." Jack retorts: "Oh, that's nonsense, Algy. You never talk
anything but nonsense." But Algernon, Wilde's spokesman here,
replies: "Nobody ever does" (*Earnest*, p. 339). No one speaks any-

thing except nonsense or is anything except trivial in Wilde's dandiacal world.

Other inversions of such romantic clichés are found in epigrams and certain conversational exchanges constructed on the principle of the reversal of our expectations. A simple example is represented by Algernon's views about marriage proposals: "I really don't see anything romantic in proposing. It is very romantic to be in love. But there is nothing romantic about a definite proposal. Why, one may be accepted" (*Earnest*, p. 323). When Algernon tells Cecily that Jack intends to send him away, her reply is similarly inverted: "It is always painful to part from people whom one has known for a very brief space of time. The absence of old friends one can endure with equanimity. But even a momentary separation from anyone to whom one has just been introduced is almost unbearable" (*Earnest*, p. 357). Such inversions are occasionally compounded in conversational exchanges. When Jack learns his real name is Earnest, Gwendolen is ecstatic. Jack, however, is apologetic: "Gwendolen, it is a terrible thing for a man to find out suddenly that all his life he has been speaking nothing but the truth. Can you forgive me?" Gwendolen's reply continues the pattern: "I can. For I feel that you are sure to change" (*Earnest*, p. 383). This exchange makes clear, perhaps better than most, the nature and purpose of Wilde's technique. In the world of the dandy, of the Bunburyist, the norm of behavior is the reverse of that of conventional society. This principle holds true for Gwendolen and Cecily as well as Jack and Algernon.

Wilde's constant reversal of our romantic expectations in stock situations and epigrammatic speech represents one of his methods of constructing a play based upon the principle that, in art, form or style is higher than representational truth or morality. Wilde supports this idea not only by the symmetry of his plot with its carefully balanced characters and situations but also by having his characters directly set forth the idea that the *form* of any activity is more important than its truth. The idea is directly stated early in the play:

Jack: . . . You don't think there is any chance of Gwendolen becoming like her mother in about a hundred and fifty years, do you, Algy?
Algernon: All women become like their mothers. That is their tragedy.
    No man does. That's his.
Jack: Is that clever?

Algernon: It is perfectly phrased! And quite as true as any observation
in civilized life should be.

(*Earnest*, p. 335)

Thus, truth, in perfect accord with Wildean artistic principles, is
subordinated to form. The idea is further amplified in the fourth act
during the scene in which Algernon and Jack explain their double
roles:

Cecily: Why did you pretend to be my guardian's brother?
Algernon: In order that I might have an opportunity of meeting you.
Cecily (to Gwendolen): That certainly seems a satisfactory explanation,
does it not?
Gwendolen: Yes, dear, if you can believe him.
Cicily: I don't. But that does not affect the wonderful beauty of
his answer.
Gwendolen: True. In matters of grave importance, style, not sincerity,
is the vital thing. Mr. Worthing, what explanation can you offer
to me for pretending to have a brother? Was it in order that
you might have an opportunity of coming up to town to see me
as often as possible?
Jack: Can you doubt it, Miss Fairfax?
Gwendolen: I have the gravest doubts upon the subject. But I intend
to crush them. This is not the moment for German scepticism.

(*Earnest*, pp. 370-371)

In such passages Wilde illustrates his skillful blending of comic
technique, artistic credo, and subtle social commentary.

Wilde's characters are constructed on similar principles and
ideas. Both Algernon and Jack are sophisticated men of the world.
The smooth, self-assured surfaces of these two Bunburyists contrast
markedly with the innocent absurdity of their actions. Thus, Eric
Bently in *The Playwright as Thinker* sees the "counterpoint of
irony" of Wilde's play expressing itself "theatrically in the contrast
between the elegance and *savoir faire* of the actors and the absurdity of what they actually do." Bentley sees this as a manisfestation of
Wilde's effort to adjust to his time: "It was the solution of
Bohemianism . . . Bohemianism was for Wilde a mask. To wear
masks was Wilde's personal adjustment to modern life, as it was
Nietzsche's."[37] But it can also be argued that this contrast between
elegant surface and absurd action in the play represents Wilde's

method of objectifying his artistic credo. Moreover, this was Wilde's way of rejecting the Victorian ideals of "earnestness" that were supposed to inform behavior. Gwendolen and Cecily, characters cut out of the same cloth as Algernon and Jack, function in much the same way. No less self-assured and certainly no less innocently absurd, their language and behavior are simply feminine parallels of Algernon and Jack's.

What, after all, is the importance of *The Importance of Being Earnest?* Jack's reply to Lady Bracknell's accusation that he is "displaying signs of triviality" does not help much. Jack replies that for the first time he has realized "the vital importance of being earnest." Beyond the obvious play on words the closing line seems to mean nothing at all. We need to remember, however, that throughout the play the dialogue has been turning conventional and "earnest" attitudes upside down. The traditional values connected with love, marriage, birth, death, sin, truth, sincerity, baptism, and so forth have been "trivialized" by means of burlesque, parody, verbal nonsense, and wit. But the term "trivial" requires redefinition. The subtitle of Wilde's play is "A Trivial Play for Serious People." If by this term Wilde means "negligible" or "inconsequential" Wilde would be applying the same standards of judgment as his Philistine critics. If by "trivial," however, we mean a susceptibility to artistic form, the delicate patterns of language, the artificial elegances of living, we come much closer to Wilde's meaning. The sort of "earnestness" that Wilde is rejecting in this play is the sort of stuffiness, priggishness, and hypocrisy that he detected in Victorian society. Wilde's drama demonstrates the dictum that "Lying, the telling of beautiful untrue things, is the proper aim of Art" ("Decay of Lying," p. 320). For example, at the end of the play Jack asks Gwendolen's forgiveness when he realizes that all of his life he has been telling the truth. Gwendolen replies that she can forgive him for she feels that he is certain to change. Jack has in reality discovered the importance of *not* being earnest. He has discovered the truth that Wilde set forth in "The Decay of Lying" and "The Critic as Artist": that just as it is "the function of literature to create, from the rough material of actual existence, a new world that will be more marvelous, more enduring, and more true than the world that common eyes look upon," so it is the function of man to create by "imaginative lying" and the cultivation of the beautiful forms of life, a personality that will realize the highest aims of art.

CHAPTER 7

De Profundis

" I was a man who stood in symbolic relations to the art and
culture of my age," Oscar Wilde asserted in his now-famous
letter to Lord Alfred Douglas. Written in 1897 in his narrow cell in
Reading Prison, Wilde's *De Profundis* represents almost the last of
his literary achievements. Only "The Ballad of Reading Gaol," con-
ceived during his imprisonment, remained to be written during the
first of his three years of life in exile. Consequently, Wilde's long
letter to his dangerous friend, later given the title "De Profundis"
by Robert Ross, is an extraordinarily interesting document to students of Wilde. Not only does Wilde attempt to assess the nature
and consequences of his friendship with Lord Alfred Douglas, but
he attempts to bring into meaningful relationship his life, career,
artistic ideas, failures, suffering, and ideas of Christ and martyrdom.
Wilde explained his purposes in a letter to More Adey written
February 18, 1897: "It is the most important letter of my life, as it
will deal ultimately with my future mental attitude toward life, with
the way in which I desire to meet the world again, with the development of my character: with what I have lost, what I have
learned, and what I hope to arrive at" (*Letters*, p. 419). From these
words and from much of *De Profundis* itself, the reader derives a
stong impression that Wilde is playing a role and is conscious of an
audience assessing the skill of his performance. The effect is sometimes insincere and contradictory, but always revealing. Here, as
elsewhere, the Wildean pose needs to be taken into account.

Wilde began his *De Profundis* letter in January of 1897. He wrote
it in his cell on a table made of his plank bed. Wilde's long letter was
written on eighty pages of blue prison paper which were doled out
one sheet at a time. When one sheet was finished, it was supposed
to be taken away and another provided.[1] Moreover, the governor of
the prison refused Wilde permission to mail the completed manu-

153

script from prison. Only after his release and subsequent meeting with Robert Ross in Dieppe was he finally able to give the manuscript to his friend and eventual literary executor. Wilde had provided elaborate instructions for its copying. A first copy was made by Ross dictating the manuscript to a typist. Copies were then made of certain parts that were to be sent to specified people. Finally, a second copy was made from the original typescript. One of these typed copies was sent to Lord Alfred Douglas.

Wilde's literary position on the Continent had not suffered as it had in England. When it came to be known that Wilde had created a literary work in prison, a Dr. Max Meyerfeld asked Ross for permission to translate and publish the letter. After much persuasion Ross consented and most of the letter appeared in a German journal in 1905. A similarly expurgated English edition was published by Methuen in 1905 and, much to Ross' surprise, was well received by the public. In November 1909 Robert Ross delivered the manuscript to the British Museum with instructions that it not be shown to the public for fifty years. However, in 1912, upon the publication of his *Oscar Wilde: A Critical Study*, Arthur Ransome revealed the identity of the intended recipient, a fact which Ross had concealed. Douglas immediately sued for libel; and it became necessary to read the manuscript, including the suppressed portions, in court. The strength of Wilde's attack upon Douglas' character no doubt made a sufficiently strong impression upon the jury, and the court ruled in Ransome's favor.[2] The manuscript was thereupon returned to the British Museum where until 1960 it did not see the light of day.[3]

The first half of *De Profundis* deals with Wilde's relationships with Lord Alfred Douglas, the young and handsome poet whom Wilde loved and supported for several years. As the following passage suggests, the tone of Wilde's letter is sometimes bitter, self-pitying, and calculated to inflict pain:

As I set here in this dark cell in convict clothes, a disgraced and ruined man, I blame myself . . . . I blame myself for allowing an unintellectual friendship, a friendship whose primary aim was not the creation and contemplation of beautiful things, to entirely dominate my life. From the very first there was too wide a gap between us. You had been idle at your school, worse than idle at your university. You did not realise that an artist, and especially such an artist as I am, one, that is to say, the quality of whose works depends on the intensification of personality, requires for the development of his art the companionship of ideas, and intellectual atmosphere, quiet, peace, and solitude. You admired my work when it was finished: you enjoyed the brilliant successes of my first nights, and the brilliant banquets that followed them: you were proud, and quite naturally so, of being the intimate friend of an artist so distinguished: but you could not understand the conditions requisite for the production of artistic work. I am not speaking in phrases of rhetorical exaggeration but in terms of absolute truth to actual fact when I remind you that during the whole time we were together I never wrote one single line. Whether at Torquay, Goring, London, Florence or elsewhere, my life, as long as you were by my side, was entirely sterile and uncreative. (*Letters*, pp. 425-426)

Much of the first half of the letter continues in this vein with Wilde blaming Lord Alfred Douglas for his "utter and discreditable" financial ruin and his "entire ethical degradation." But he closes his long letter with the suggestion that some good has come from their friendship after all: "You came to me to learn the Pleasure of Life and the Pleasure of Art. Perhaps I am chosen to teach you something much more wonderful, the meaning of Sorrow, and its beauty" (*Letters*, p. 511).

Wilde's real concern, however, seems to be with the problem of fitting the present circumstances of his life into his artistic scheme, especially the role of suffering in self-development. In "The Critic as Artist" and "The Soul of Man Under Socialism" Wilde had explained the importance of self-development in life. But in these earlier works self-development in life consisted only of developing one's unique personality, as Lord Henry Wotton revealed in his conversations with Dorian Gray: "The aim of life is self-development. To realise one's nature perfectly—that is what each of us is here for" (*Dorian Gray*, p. 39). But such development has nothing whatever to do with pain or suffering as Lord Henry, Dorian's mentor and Wilde's spokesman, insists: "I can sympathise with everything, except suffering . . . . I cannot sympathise with that. It is too ugly, too horrible, too distressing. There is something terribly morbid in the modern sympathy with pain. One should sympathise with the colour, the beauty, the joy of life" (*Dorian Gray*, p. 44). By the time Wilde had written *De Profundis*, his ideas had changed. He still believed that for the artistic "life is simple self-development" (*Letters*, p. 476), but he sees himself at a "starting point for a fresh development" (*Letters*, p. 467) now that he has suffered:

I now see that sorrow, being the supreme emotion of which man is capable, is at once the type and test of all great Art. What the artist is always looking for is that mode of existence in which soul and body are one and indivisible: in which the outward is expressive of the inward: in which Form reveals. . . . Truth in Art is the unity of a thing with itself: the outward rendered expressive of the inward: the soul made incarnate: the body instinct with spirit. For this reason there is no truth comparable to Sorrow. There are times when Sorrow seems to me to be the only truth. Other things may be illusions of the eye or the appetite, made to blind the one and cloy the other, but out of Sorrow have the worlds been built, and at the birth of a child or a star there is pain. (*Letters*, p. 473)

Where once beauty and the myriad sensations of life served as the raw materials for the artistic life, now suffering and pain serve as the media for the shaping of the artistic personality. From this new aesthetic source, Wilde predicted something new: "Perhaps there may come into my art also, no less than into my life, a still deeper note, one of greater unity of passion, and directness of impulse. Not width but intensity is the true aim of modern Art" (*Letters*, p. 489). Wilde achieved exactly what he anticipated, for his last work, "The Ballad of Reading Gaol," is indeed distinguished by its intensity, stark simplicity, and high seriousness.

Although Wilde revealed his fascination with the figure of Christ in one form or another throughout his literary career, only in *De Profundis* did he actually make him a part of his aesthetic system— especially his conception of the artistic personality. Wilde saw an "intimate and immediate connection between the true life of Christ and the true life of the artist" (*Letters*, p. 476). The significant connection derives from the fact that ". . . we can discern in Christ that close union of personality with perfection which forms the real distinction between classical and romantic Art and makes Christ the true precursor of the romantic movement in life . . ." (*Letters*, p. 476). Christ's incarnation represented for Wilde a kind of incarnation of the artistic perfection of self that is the aim of Wilde's notion of self-development. Hence, Christ is "the most supreme of Individualists" who taught us that "the history of each separate individual is, or can be made, the history of the world" (*Letters*, p. 480). The chief struggle of Christ, and Wilde, was against the "dull lifeless mechanical systems that treat people as if they were things, and so treat everybody alike. . . ." (*Letters*, p. 485). The same Philistinism that Matthew Arnold attacked in *Culture and Anarchy* and Wilde ridiculed in his comedies, Christ, as the precursor of Romanticism, fought against two thousand years earlier:

That is the war every child of light has to wage. Philistinism was the note of the age and communty in which he lived. In their heavy inacessibility to ideas, their dull respectability, their tedious orthodoxy, their worship of vulgar success, their entire preoccupation with the gross materialistic side of life, and their ridiculous estimate of themselves and their importance, the Jew of Jerusalem in Christ's day was the exact counterpart of the British Philistine of our own. (*Letters*, pp. 485-486)

Christ is envisioned, however, in highly Wildean terms, for "in a manner not yet understood of the world he regarded sin and suffering as being in themselves beautiful, holy things, and modes of perfection. It *sounds* a very dangerous idea. It is so. All great ideas are dangerous" (*Letters*, p. 486). Wilde unites in the figure of Christ not only himself and his distaste for Philistinism but the various elements of his aesthetic at the core of which is his theory of personality. Each of us must strive, through the cultivation of our potentialities for Individualism, to become the embodiment of the perfection of art. Wilde in his earlier writings urged us to reach toward this perfection by cultivating our sense of beauty, but now this goal is to be reached through suffering and sorrow. This is what Wilde means when he speaks of "that close unity of personality with perfection" that Christ alone achieved.

Wilde suggests that the two turning points in his life took place when his father sent him to Oxford and when society sent him to prison. At Oxford the major influence in his life was Walter Pater, and Wilde seems to imply that "Pater's *Renaissance*—that book which had such a strange influence over my life" (*Letters*, p. 471)—was partly responsible for his tragedy. He recalled telling one of his friends at Oxford, while under the influence of Pater, that he "wanted to eat of the fruit of all the trees in the garden of the world" (*Letters*, p. 475). But from his prison cell the Paterian injunction now seemed a dangerous one: "People whose desire is solely for self-realisation never know where they are going" (*Letters*, p. 488). Wilde never denies the validity of his theory of self-development; he only wishes to affirm that it can just as readily lead to personal destruction as personal realization. Wilde does not hesitate to admit in *De Profundis* that, although the gods had given him everything, he had taken poor care of his talent: "I let myself be lured into long spells of senseless and sensual ease. I amused myself with being a *flâneur*, a dandy, a man of fashion. I surrounded myself with the smaller natures and the meaner minds. I became the spendthrift of my own genius, and to waste an eternal youth gave me a curious joy. Tired of being on the heights I deliberately went to the depths in the search for new sensations" (*Letters*, p. 466).

Few writers have had the opportunity of assessing their lives and artistic careers from the peculiar vantage point that Wilde was provided, albeit tragically, by his trial, financial and social ruin, and imprisonment. *De Profundis* represents an effort to come to terms with what had been, was, and was to be. It represented Wilde's effort at personal survival. Its syntheses, contradictions, and even its insincerities need to be seen in that light to be understood.[4] When Wilde says that he was "a man who stood in symbolic relations" to the art and culture of his age, he is essentially correct, for in Wilde the artist and Wilde the personality were embodied the main intellectual and artistic currents of his time.

Notes and References

Chapter One

1. Oscar Wilde, *The Letters of Oscar Wilde*, ed. Rupert Hart-Davis (New York: Harcourt, Brace & World, Inc., 1962), p. 466. Further references to this edition of Wilde's letters will be indicated parenthetically in the text by *Letters* followed by page numbers.

2. According to Vyvyan Holland, Oscar's second son, Jane's hand can be seen in the choice of these names. Oscar was the son of Ossian, the third-century Irish warrior-bard. Fingal was Ossian's father. O'Flahertie represented some supposed or real connection with "the ferocious O'Flaherties of Galyway." Wills was a family name of the Wildes (*Oscar Wilde: A Pictorial Biography* (New York: The Viking Press, 1960), p. 12.

3. Hesketh Pearson, *Oscar Wilde: His Life and Wit* (New York: Harper and Bros., 1946), p. 6.

4. The biographers differ as to the date of Oscar's birth: Hesketh Pearson (p. 8) gives 1856 as the year of Wilde's birth; Philippe Jullian (*Oscar Wilde*, trans. by Violet Wyndham (London: Constable, 1969), p. 13, offers 1855; even the *Dictionary of National Biography* offers 1856 as the date of Wilde's birth. Robert Harborough Sherard, *The Life of Oscar Wilde* (London: T. Werner Laurie, 1911), p. 75, provides the correct date of 1854.

5. Wilde's biographers all mention this: R. H. Sherard, p. 75; Boris Brasol, *Oscar Wilde: The Man—The Artist—The Martyr* (New York: Charles Scribner's Sons, 1938), p. 19; Frances Winwar, p. 11; Hesketh Pearson, p. 15; Philippe Jullian, p. 20.

6. Philippe Jullian, p. 13.

7. Hesketh Pearson, p. 19.

8. Lloyd Lewis and Henry Justin Smith, *Oscar Wilde Discovers America* (New York: Harcourt Brace and Company, 1936), p. 162.

9. Hesketh Pearson, p. 25.

10. Lloyd Lewis and Henry Justin Smith, p. 162.

11. Hesketh Pearson, p. 31.

12. Jerome Hamilton Buckley, *The Victorian Temper* (Cambridge: Harvard University Press, 1969), p. 216.

13. Charles Frederick Harrold and William D. Templeman, *English Prose of the Victorian Era* (New York: Oxford University Press, 1938), p. LXXVI.

14. The term means "end of the century." It has been often applied to the last ten years of the nineteenth century, a period when writers and other artists were consciously abandoning old ideas and conventions and attempting to discover new ones. Wilde himself used the term in *A Woman of No Importance*, in *The Picture of Dorian Gray*, and in his letters. See Holbrook Jackson, *The Eighteen-Nineties* (New York: Capricorn, 1966), pp. 17-32.

15. Donald H. Ericksen, "Harold Skimpole: Dickens and the Early 'Art for Art's Sake' Movement," *Journal of English and Germanic Philology*, 72 (January 1973), p. 58.

16. Buckley pp. 224-225.

17. Hesketh Pearson, p. 42.

18. Hesketh Pearson, p. 59.

19. Ibid., p. 82.

20. *Dublin University Magazine* 90 (July 1877), pp. 118-126.

21. "Mr. Whistler's Ten O'Clock," *Pall Mall Gazette*, 41 (February 21, 1885), p. 2.

22. Hesketh Pearson, p. 199.

23. Lord Alfred Douglas, *The Autobiography of Lord Alfred Douglas*, New Edition (New York: Books for Libraries Press, 1931), pp. 75-76.

24. Hesketh Pearson, p. 243. See *Letters*, p. 326, 326n.

25. Ibid., p. 248.

26. H. Montgomery Hyde, *Oscar Wilde: The Aftermath* (London: Methuen & Co. Ltd., 1963), pp. 3-10.

27. The Governor of Reading Gaol during the last half of Wilde's imprisonment did much to make Wilde's prison life, as well as that of the other prisoners, more bearable. In gratitude Wilde sent him a copy of "The Ballad of Reading Gaol" when it appeared (H. Montgomery Hyde, pp. 78-80).

28. The original dedication of "The Ballad of Reading Gaol" expressed his gratitude to Ross: "When I came out of prison some met me with garments and with spices and others with wise counsel. You met me with love" (Stuart Mason, *Bibliography of Oscar Wilde*, New Edition (London: Bertram Rota, 1967), p. 408.

Chapter Two

1. Edouard Roditi, *Oscar Wilde*, (Norfolk, Connecticut: New Directions, 1947), p. 25.

2. The term "Impressionism" is borrowed from painting and refers to the art techniques of Monet, Degas, Renoir, and others. Literary Impressionism holds that the presentation of the literary object as it is seen or felt

by the artist in a passing moment is of more importance than precise detail or realistic finish. Just as the Impressionistic painter would be concerned with the effects of light, a few brush strokes of pure color, and ephemeral outdoor scenes, so the literary Impressionist would employ selective details and a few "brush strokes" of sensory data to suggest the effect upon him. Wilde's "Impression du Matin" is an excellent example of literary Impressionism.

3. See Stephen von Ullmann, "Synasthesien in den dichterischen Werken von Oscar Wilde," *Englische Studien*, 72 (Leipzig 1938), pp. 245–256.

4. Jerome H. Buckley, p. 234.

5. Oscar Wilde, "Ravenna," *Complete Works of Oscar Wilde* (London: Collins, 1968), vol. 11, 30-32; Further references to Wilde's poems, fiction, and drama from this edition will be indicated parenthetically in the text by title and line or page numbers.

6. Edouard Roditi, "Oscar Wilde's Poetry as Art History," *Poetry*, 67 (1946), p. 334.

7. Boris Brasol, *Oscar Wilde: The Man—The Artist—The Martyr* (New York: Charles Scribner's Sons, 1938), p. 72.

8. Epifanio San Juan, Jr., *The Art of Oscar Wilde* (Princeton: Princeton University Press, 1967), p. 23.

9. Arthur Ransome, *Oscar Wilde: A Critical Study* (London: Methuen, 1912), p. 38.

10. Hesketh Pearson, *Oscar Wilde: His Life and Wit*, pp. 45-46.

11. Ibid., p. 46.

12. Unsigned review, *Spectator*, 54 (August 13, 1881), p. 1049.

13. Unsigned review, *Athenaeum* (July 23, 1881), p. 104.

14. Unsigned review, *Saturday Review*, 52 (July 23, 1881), p. 118.

15. J. D. Thomas, "Oscar Wilde's Pose and Poetry," *Rice Institute Pamphlets*, 42 (1954), p. 39.

16. Hesketh Pearson, p. 46.

17. Stuart Mason, *Bibliography of Oscar Wilde*, New Edition (London: Bertram Rota, 1967), p. 289.

18. In a letter written to W. B. Yeats in August or September of 1894, Wilde said "I don't know that I think Requiescat very typical of my work" (*Letters*, p. 365).

19. Stuart Mason, p. 305.

20. Unsigned notice, *Saturday Review*, 52 (July 23, 1881), p. 118.

21. Arthur Ransome, pp. 54-55.

22. See G. Wilson Knight, *The Christian Renaissance* (London: Methuen, 1962), pp. 287-300.

23. Oscar Wilde, "Mr. Whistler's Ten O'Clock," *Pall Mall Gazette* 41 (February 21, 1885), pp. 1-2; reprinted in *The Artist as Critic: The Critical Writings of Oscar Wilde*, ed. Richard Ellmann (New York: Vintage, 1970), p. 15. Further references to Wilde's criticism for this edition will be indicated parenthetically in the text.

24. J. D. Thomas, "The Composition of Wilde's 'The Harlot's House,' " 65 *Modern Language Notes* (November 1950), p. 486.

25. Roditi, *Oscar Wilde*, p. 231.

26. J. D. Thomas, "The Composition of Wilde's 'The Harlot's House,' " p. 486.

27. Stuart Mason, p. 399.

28. Ibid., p. 398.

29. Roditi, *Oscar Wilde*, p. 25.

30. San Juan, Jr., p. 32.

31. Hyde, *Oscar Wilde: The Aftermath*, p. 67.

32. *Reading Mercury*, July 10, 1896, cited by Stuart Mason, p. 426.

33. "Expressionism" refers to the tendency in art to abandon the representation of objects realistically in favor of distorting them in order to convey the impressions or moods of a character or the artist himself. Unlike the Impressionist, the Expressionist achieves his effects not so much by the selection of details as by their distortion and exaggeration. The term is usually associated with the theater of the 1920s.

34. Vincent O'Sullivan, *Aspects of Wilde* (New York: Henry Holt, 1936), p. 97. See *Letters*, pp. 630-631, for Wilde's characterization of Smithers.

35. Oscar Wilde occupied prison cell three on the third landing of Gallery C.

36. The original dedication was as follows: "When I came out of prison some met me with garments and with spices and others with wise counsel. You met me with love" (Stuart Mason, p. 408).

37. Ibid., pp. 407-427.

38. Hesketh Pearson, p. 308.

39. Roditi, "Oscar Wilde's Poetry as Art History," p. 330.

40. Jerome H. Buckley, *The Victorian Temper* (Cambridge: Harvard University, 1969), p. 234.

Chapter Three

1. Hesketh Pearson, *Oscar Wilde: His Life and Wit* (New York: Harper and Bros., 1946), p. 117.

2. Wilde's reaction (see *Letters*, pp. 299-302) to the reviews of *The Speaker* (November 28, 1892) and the *Pall Mall Gazette* (November 30, 1891) suggests strongly that he felt his *A House of Pomegranates* represented significant art.

3. Walter Pater, *Letters*, p. 219n.

4. See G. Wilson Knight, *The Christian Renaissance* (London: Methuen, 1962), pp. 287-300; and Pearson, *Oscar Wilde* pp. 120-121.

5. Pearson, p. 118.

6. Roditi, *Oscar Wilde*, p. 104.

7. Pearson, p. 117.

8. Ransome, *Oscar Wilde: A Critical Study*, p. 108.

9. Roditi, *Oscar Wilde*, p. 104.

10. Unsigned notice, *Athenaeum* (September 1, 1888), p. 286.

11. [Alexander Galt Ross], *Saturday Review*, 66 (October 20, 1888), p. 472.

12. See note 4 above.

13. *Dublin University Magazine*, 90 (July 1877), pp. 118-126.

14. Michael Brooks, "Oscar Wilde, Charles Ricketts, and the Art of the Book," *Criticism*, 12 (Fall 1970), p. 309.

15. Unsigned review, *Pall Mall Gazette*, (November 30, 1891), p. 3.

16. Unsigned review, *Saturday Review*, 73 (February 6, 1891), p. 160.

17. Unsigned review, *The Speaker* (November 28, 1891), p. 648, in Stuart Mason, *Bibliography of Oscar Wilde*, New Edition (London: Bertram Rota, 1967), p. 365.

18. G. Wilson Knight, *The Christian Renaissance* (London: Methuen, 1962), p. 290.

Chapter Four

1. Graham Hough, *The Last Romantics* (London, Methuen, 1961), p. 203.

2. Buckley, *The Victorian Temper* , p. 228.

3. René Wellek, *A History of Modern Criticism: 1750–1950* (New Haven: Yale University Press, 1965), p. 412. The term "romanticism" is protean in its ambiguity, and critical history is replete with more or less successful attempts to define it: See René Wellek, "The Concept of Romanticism in Literary History" in *Concepts of Criticism*, ed. Stephen G. Nichols, Jr. (New Haven: Yale University Press, 1963), pp. 128-198. I use the term for my purposes in this book as C. Hugh Holman defines it: "a literary and philosophical theory which tends to see the individual at the very center of all life and all experience, and it places him, therefore, at the center of art, making literature most valuable as an expression of his unique feelings and particular attitudes . . . and valuing its accuracy in portraying his experiences, however fragmentary and incomplete, more than it values its adherence to completeness, unity, or the demands of genre. It places a high premium upon the creative function of the imagination, seeing art as a formulation of intuitive imaginative perceptions that tend to speak a nobler truth than that of fact, logic, or the here and now" (*A Handbook to Literature*, Third Edition (Indianapolis: The Odyssey Press, 1972), p. 468). This definition is not completely satisfactory for we need to add that Wilde also has ties with the great idealist tradition that art achieves its perfection in the unity of form and content. Wilde further emphasizes objectivity rather than subjectivity for he argued that "all bad poetry springs from genuine feeling."

4. The term "Decadence," as I use it here and elsewhere, refers to that period in English literary history from about the last decade of the

nineteenth century to the first decade of the twentieth. The salient characteristics of the "literature of decadence," according to Richard A. Long and
Iva G. Jones, are (1) the attenuation of emotion and the detailed analysis of
it, (2) themes of ennui, frustration, and moral confusion, (3) a general
temper that is static, (4) a treatment of the leisured classes in a highly
mannered fashion, (5) an emphasis upon form, not only in structure, but
especially in language ("Towards a Definition of the 'Decadent Novel,' "
College English, 22 (January 1961), pp. 245-249).

   5. Richard Ellmann, "Introduction: The Critic as Artist as Wilde," *The
Artist as Critic: Critical Writings of Oscar Wilde* (New York: Vintage, 1970),
x.

   6. San Juan, Jr., *The Art of Oscar Wilde*, p. 102.

   7. The four essays published as *Intentions* in 1891 had all been published separately: The first essay appeared as "The Decay of Lying: A
dialogue," *Nineteenth Century*, 25 (January 1889), pp. 35-56; the second as
"Pen, Pencil and Poison: A study," *Fortnightly*, 45 N.S. (January 1, 1889),
pp. 41-54; the two-part "Critic as Artist" appeared as "The True Function
and Value of Criticism; With Some Remarks on the Importance of Doing
Nothing: A Dialogue," *Nineteenth Century*, (July, September 1890), pp.
123-147, 435-459; "The Truth of Masks" appeared as "Shakespeare and
Stage Costume," *Nineteenth Century*, 17 (May 1895), pp. 800-818. All of
these essays were revised when collected.

   8. Cyril and Vivian were the names of Wilde's two sons born in 1885
and 1886, respectively.

   9. Lewis Mumford, *The Myth of the Machine: Technics and Human
Development* (New York: Harcourt Brace, 1966) p. 78.

   10. Lord Lytton, "Mary Anderson's Juliet," *Nineteenth Century* (December 1884).

   11. The version that appeared in Blackwood's was later expanded from
twelve thousand to twenty-six thousand words (Vyvyan Holland, *The Portrait of Mr. W. H.* by Oscar Wilde (London: Methuen, 1957), xii.)

   12. The Willie Hughes theory was first advanced in 1766 by a Shakespearean scholar named Thomas Tyrwhitt (Vyvyan Holland, p. ix).

   13. The dedication is subject to myriad interpretations depending upon
how you choose to punctuate.

   14. Like the fictitious Cyril Graham, Wilde had a portrait of Willie
Hughes painted (in the style of Francois Clouet) by Charles Ricketts on a
piece of decayed oak who then framed it in worm-eaten wood (Jean Paul
Raymond and Charles Ricketts, *Recollections* (Bloomsbury: Nonesuch Press
1932), pp. 35–36.)

   15. Pearson, *Oscar Wilde*, p. 142.

   16. Ibid., p. 141. It is an interesting and possibly relevant fact that
Wilde's signature was the only one that G. B. Shaw was able to obtain for a
reprieve of the Chicago Haymarket anarchists.

17. Ibid., p. 141.

18. Masolino D'Amico, "Oscar Wilde Between Socialism and Aestheticism," *English Miscellany*, 18 (1967), p. 118.

19. Brian Nicholas, "Two Nineteenth-Century Utopias: The Influence of Renan's 'L'Avenir de la science' on Wilde's 'The Soul of Man Under Socialism,' " *Modern Language Review*, 59 (1964), pp. 361-370.

Chapter Five

1. See H. Lucius Cook, "French Sources of Wilde's *Picture of Dorian Gray*," *Romanic Review*, 19 (1929), pp. 29-30.

2. Dominick Rossi, "Parallels in Wilde's *The Picture of Dorian Gray and* Goethe's *Faust*," *College Language Association Journal*, 13 (1969), pp. 188-191.

3. Roditi, *Oscar Wilde* , p. 114. It is interesting to note that Goethe attempted a translation of Maturin's novel. See L. A. Willoughby, "Oscar Wilde and Goethe: The Life of Art and the Art of Life," *Publications of the English Goethe Society*, 35 (1964-65), p. 4.

4. [Samuel Henry Jeyes], "A study in Puppydom," *St. James Gazette* (June 24, 1890), p. 4.

5. Unsigned review, *Daily Chronicle* (June 30, 1890), p. 7.

6. Walter Pater, "A Novel by Mr. Oscar Wilde," *Bookman*, 1 (November 1891), p. 59.

7. Other critics have recognized a parallel to the Temptation and Fall. Ted Spivey argues that ". . . the root cause of Dorian's damnation as well as the source of Harry's evil is an insatiable curiosity, a never-ending desire for knowledge." This curiosity and art leads to "the inevitable and complete egoism, which is only another word for damnation" ("Damnation and Salvation in *The Picture of Dorian Gray*," *Boston University Studies in English*, 4 (1961), pp. 163-169); Richard Ellmann maintains that "Dorian sells his soul not to the devil but, in the ambiguous form of his portrait, to art: ("Romantic Pantomine in Oscar Wilde," *Partisan Review*, 30 (1963), p. 353); Epifanio San Juan, Jr. sees Hallward in the role of the Creator: "When he kills Hallward, he denies the creator of his beauty; for the painter is solely responsible for his preternatural beauty and his vanity. Just as Adam denies his Creator, so Dorian commits the 'sin' of pride" *The Art of Oscar Wilde* (Princeton: Princeton University Press, 1967), p. 52.

8. See Jan B. Gordon, "Parody as Imitation: The Sad Education of Dorian Gray," *Criticism*, 9 (Fall 1967), pp. 355-71.

9. Roditi, p. 183.

10. Richard Ellmann notes that "The painter Hallward has little of Ruskin at the beginning, but gradually he moves closer to that pillar of esthetic taste and moral judgment upon which Wilde leaned, and after Hallward is safely murdered, Dorian with sudden fondness recollects a trip they had made to Venice together, when his friend was captivated by Tintorett's art.

Ruskin was of course the English discoverer and champion of Tintoretto, so that the illusion is not vague" ("Overtures to Wilde's Salome," *Tri-Quarterly*, 15 (Spring 1969), p. 59.

11. Houston A. Baker, Jr., "A Tragedy of the Artist: *The Picture of Dorian Gray*," *Nineteenth Century Fiction*, 24 (1969), p. 353.

12. William E. Portnoy, "Wilde's Debt to Tennyson in Dorian Gray," *English Literature in Transition*, 17 (1974), pp. 259-261.

13. John Pappas, "The Flower and the Beast: A Study of Oscar Wilde's Antithetical Attitudes Towards Nature and Man in *The Picture of Dorian Gray*," *English Literature in Transition*, 15 (1972), No. 1, pp. 37-48.

14. Jan B. Gordon, "Parody as Imitation," pp. 355-371.

15. Ibid., p. 359.

16. San Juan, p. 56.

17. San Juan presents a similar argument: "The novel portrays the attempt of a young man to transcend the flux of temporal experience" (*The Art of Oscar Wilde*, p. 59).

18. Roditi, p. 124.

19. San Juan, p. 50.

20. Ibid., p. 67.

21. The varieties of interpretations of the meaning of the portrait and its degeneration are almost endless. See L. A. Willoughby, "Oscar Wilde and Goethe: The Life of Art and the Art of Life," p. 9; "The Rage of Caliban," *University of Toronto Quarterly*, 37 (October 1967), p. 84; Alick West, "Walter Pater and Oscar Wilde," *The Mountain in the Sunlight: Studies in Conflict* (London: Laurence and Wishart, 1958), p. 138; Jan B. Gordon, "Parody as Imitation: The Sad Education of Dorian Gray," *Criticism*, 9 (Fall 1967), p. 355; Epifanio San Juan, Jr, *The Art of Oscar Wilde*, p. 50; Houston A. Baker, Jr., "A Tragedy of the Artist: *The Picture of Dorian Gray*," *Nineteenth Century Fiction*, 24 (1969), p. 355.

22. Unless we see the rejection of Wilde's artistic credo as an immoral act, it is difficult to see any effort by Wilde to undercut Lord Henry. Richard Ellmann even argues that because Dorian adopts Wilde's artistic views he necessarily comes to grief: "Dorian, falling under Lord Henry's Mephistopheleon tutelage, takes seriously what Lord Henry takes lightly, shows Wilde's too often stated preference for art over life, and of course comes to grief with it. Estheticism, embraced as a new gospel, becomes diabolical, just as life, seen as all in all, becomes boring" ("Overtones to Wilde's Salome," *Tri-Quarterly*, 15 (Spring 1969), p. 353.

23. Alick West, p. 137.

24. Jacob Korg, "The Rage of Caliban," *University of Toronto Quarterly*, 37 (October 1967), p. 89.

Chapter Six

1. Richard Ellmann, "Overtures to Wilde's Salome," *Tri-Quarterly*, 15 (Spring 1969), p. 46.

2. Morris Freedman, "The Modern Tragicomedy of Wilde and O'Casey," *College English*, 25 (April 1964), p. 527.

3. Boris Brasol, *Oscar Wilde: The Man—The Artist—The Martyr*, (New York: Charles Scribner, 1938), p. 87.

4. Hesketh Pearson, *Oscar Wilde: His Life and His Wit*, (New York: Harper and Brothers, 1946), p. 48.

5. Unsigned review, *New York Times* (August 21, 1883), p. 5.

6. Frances Winwar, p. 120.

7. Stuart Mason, *Bibliography of Oscar Wilde*, New Edition (London: Bertram Rota, 1967), p. 327.

8. Hesketh Pearson, p. 71; and Frances Winwar, p. 113.

9. Hesketh Pearson, p. 200.

10. Wilde disliked Beardsley and his illustrations for *Salome:* "They are cruel and evil, and so like dear Aubrey, who has a face like a silver hatchet, with grass-green hair" (Pearson, p. 204).

11. Hesketh Pearson, p. 202.

12. Stuart Mason, p. 373.

13. Unsigned notice, *The Times* (February 23, 1893), p. 8.

14. Unsigned review, *Pall Mall Gazette* (February 27, 1893), p. 3.

15. William Archer, "Mr. Oscar Wilde's New Play," *Black and White*, 4 (May 11, 1893), p. 290. When *Salome* was censored in England William Archer wrote a strong letter of protest in the *Pall Mall Gazette* on July 1, 1892 in which he termed the English censor the "Great Irresponsible" (see *Letters*, p. 317n). He was the only witness to appear before the Select Committee of the House of Commons in 1892 to advocate the abolition of censorship.

16. Z. Raafat, "The Literary Indebtedness of Wilde's *Salome* to Sardou's *Theodora, "Revue de Litterature Comparee*, 40 (1966), pp. 453-466. See also Richard Ellmann "Overtures to Wilde's *Salome*," p. 46.

17. See San Juan, Jr., *The Art of Oscar Wilde*, p. 120.

18. Joris Karl Huysmans, *Against the Grain* (New York: Illustrated Edition Company, 1931), p. 141.

19. San Juan, Jr., p. 123.

20. Richard Ellmann, "Overtures to Wilde's *Salome*, p. 60.

21. Edouard Roditi, *Oscar Wilde* (Norfolk, Connecticut: New Directions Books, 1947), p. 44.

22. Clement Scott, "Lady Windermere's Fan," *Illustrated London News*, 100 (February 27, 1892), p. 278.

23. A. B. Walkley, "Lady Windermere's Fan," *Speaker*, 5 (February 27, 1892), p. 258.

24. Arthur Ganz sees a concern for form as the essential quality in the dandy: "Above all, the Wildean dandy is the advocate of the supremacy of artistic form. It was his religion, however inadequate as such, and to Wilde art meant perfect form. The content, particularly the moral content, of the work was irrelevant; form was everything. The great dandiacal joke which

appears over and over again in the plays is based on the exaltation of the external, or formal, over the internal. The world of the dandy is based on manners not on morals" ("The Dandiacal Drama: A Study of the Plays of Oscar Wilde," *Dissertation Abstracts*, 18 (April-June 1958), p. 1429.

25. Ian Gregor, "Comedy and Oscar Wilde," *Sewanee Review*, 74 (Spring 1966), p. 504.

26. Morse Peckham, "What Did Lady Windermere Learn?" *College English*, 18 (October 1956), p. 13.

27. Hesketh Pearson, *Oscar Wilde: His Life and Wit*, p. 210.

28. Frank Harris, *Oscar Wilde* (East Lansing: Michigan State University Press, 1959), p. 107.

29. Hesketh Pearson, *Oscar Wilde*, p. 218.

30. Henry James, *Letters of Henry James*, I, ed. Percy Lubbock (New York: Octagon Books, 1920), p. 233. Another American literary figure, William Dean Howells, thought *An Ideal Husband* "not only an excellent piece of art but all *(sic)* excellent piece of sense" ("The Play and the Problem", *Harper's Weekly*, 29 (March 30, 1895), p. 294.

31. Robert Harborough Sherard, *The Life of Oscar Wilde* (London: T. Werner Laurie, 1911), p. 296.

32. Hamilton Fyfe, "The Importance of Being Earnest," *New York Times* (February 17, 1895), p. 1.

33. William Archer, "The Importance of Being Earnest," *World* (February 20, 1895), pp. 55-60.

34. A. B. Walkley, "The Importance of Being Earnest," *Speaker*, 4 (February 23, 1895), p. 212.

35. George Bernard Shaw, "The Importance of Being Earnest," *Saturday Review*, 79 (February 23, 1895), p. 250.

36. Richard Foster, "Wilde as Parodist: A Second Look at the Importance of Being Earnest," *College English*, 18 (October 1956), p. 20.

37. Eric Bentley, *The Playwright as Thinker* (New York: Reynal and Hitchcock, 1947), pp. 172-177.

Chapter Seven

1. H. Montgomery Hyde, *Oscar Wilde: The Aftermath* (London: Methuen, 1963), p. 88.

2. Ibid., p. 195.

3. Ibid., pp. 197-198.

4. Joseph Butwin, "The Martyr Clown: Oscar Wilde in *De Profundis*," *Victorian Newsletter*, 42 (Fall 1972), pp. 1-6.

Selected Bibliography

PRIMARY SOURCES

ELLMANN, RICHARD, ed. *The Artist as Critic: Critical Writings of Oscar Wilde.* New York: Random House, 1969.

HART-DAVIS, RUPERT, ed. *The Letters of Oscar Wilde.* New York: Harcourt, Brace & World, 1962.

HOLLAND, VYVYAN, ed. *Complete Works of Oscar Wilde.* London and Glasgow: Collins, 1948.

SECONDARY SOURCES

AUDEN, W. H. "An Improbable Life." *New Yorker,* 39 (March 9, 1963), pp. 155-177. Very useful and interesting review article of the Rupert Hart-Davis edition of Wilde's letters.

BECKSON, KARL, ed. *Oscar Wilde: The Critical Heritage.* New York: Barnes and Noble, 1970. A useful collection of mostly contemporary and early critical responses to Wilde and his work.

CROFT-CROOKE, RUPERT. *The Unrecorded Life of Oscar Wilde.* New York: McKay, 1972. An account of Wilde's life that attempts to correct such distorted or inaccurate biographies as those of Frank Harris, Robert Sherard, and André Gide.

DOUGLAS, LORD ALFRED. *Oscar Wilde and Myself.* New York: Duffield & Co., 1914. Lord Alfred Douglas' somewhat defensive account of his friendship with Oscar Wilde.

ELLMANN, RICHARD. "Overtures to Wilde's *Salome.*" *Tri-Quarterly,* 15 (Spring 1969), pp. 45-64. Good study of Wilde's drama and the influence of Pater and Ruskin.

ELLMANN, RICHARD, ed. *Oscar Wilde: A Collection of Critical Essays.* Twentieth Century Views. Englewood Cliffs, N.J.: Prentice-Hall, 1969. A useful collection of essays on Wilde's life and art.

ELLMANN, RICHARD. "Romantic Pantomine in Oscar Wilde." *Partisan Review,* 30 (Fall 1963), pp. 342-355. Useful study of Wilde's views of art in relation to his life and works.

FIDO, MARTIN. *Oscar Wilde.* London: Hamlyn, 1973. A lavishly illustrated and interesting anecdotal account of Wilde's life and works.

GANZ, ARTHUR. "The Dandiacal Drama: A Study of the Plays of Oscar Wilde." Dissertation, Columbia University, 1958. An excellent study of Wilde's drama and his theory of art.

HARDWICK, JOHN M. D. *The Drake Guide to Oscar Wilde*. New York: Drake, 1973. A useful guide for undergraduate students containing lists of characters and summaries of the works.

HARRIS, FRANK. *Oscar Wilde: Including My Memories of Oscar Wilde* by George Bernard Shaw. East Lansing: Michigan State University Press, 1959. An interesting but unreliable account of Wilde's life and career.

HOLLAND, VYVYAN. *Oscar Wilde: A Pictorial Biography*. New York: The Viking Press, 1960. A delightful pictorial account of Wilde's life and times by his son.

HYDE, H. MONTGOMERY. *Oscar Wilde: The Aftermath*. London: Methuen & Co. Ltd., 1963. A useful account of Wilde's prison experiences and his activities following his release.

JULLIAN, PHILIPPE. *Oscar Wilde*. Translated by Violet Wyndham. London: Constable & Co. Ltd., 1969. The most recent biography.

KNIGHT, G. WILSON. *The Christian Renaissance, with Interpretations of Dante, Shakespeare and Goethe, and New Discussions of Oscar Wilde and The Gospel of Thomas*. London: Methuen & Co. Ltd., 1962. Provides interesting insights into the significance of the Christ figure in Wilde's works.

LEWIS, LLOYD, and SMITH, HENRY J. *Oscar Wilde Discovers America* (1882). New York: Harcourt Brace, 1936. Interesting anecdotal account of Wilde's trip to America.

MASON, STUART. *Bibliography of Oscar Wilde*. New Edition. London: Bertram Rota, 1967. Exhaustive and indispensable bibliography of Wilde's works.

NASSAAR, CHRISTOPHER S. *Into the Demon Universe: A Literary Exploration of Oscar Wilde*. New York: Yale University Press, 1974. A full-length study of Wilde's art, especially the later aspects, that stresses the demonic or darker elements.

PARKER, DAVID. "Oscar Wilde's Great Farce: *The Importance of Being Earnest*". *Modern Language Quarterly*, 35 (June 1974), pp. 173-186. An interesting study of the relationship of Wilde's characterization to modern themes.

PEARSON, HESKETH. *Oscar Wilde: His Life and Wit*. New York: Harper & Brothers, 1946. The fullest and most satisfactory account of Oscar Wilde's life.

RANSOME, ARTHUR. *Oscar Wilde: A Critical Study*. 3rd ed. London: Methuen and Co. Ltd., 1913. The first full-length critical study of Wilde's works.

RODITI, EDOUARD. *Oscar Wilde*. Norfolk, Connecticut: New Directions,

SAN JUAN, JR., EPIFANIO. *The Art of Oscar Wilde.* Princeton: Princeton University Press, 1967. Very good recent critical study of Wilde's works, especially the poetry.

SHERARD, ROBERT. *The Life of Oscar Wilde.* London: T. Werner Laurie, 1906. The first biography of Oscar Wilde.

SUSSMAN, HERBERT. "Criticism as Art: Form in Oscar Wilde's Critical Writings." *Studies in Philology*, 70 (Jan. 1973), pp. 108-122. An insightful study of the importance of the form in which Wilde's critical ideas are expressed.

SYMONS, ARTHUR. *A Study of Oscar Wilde.* London: Charles J. Sawyer, 1930. A relatively brief but important critical study of Wilde's art and aesthetic ideas.

WINWAR, FRANCES. *Oscar Wilde and the Yellow Nineties.* New York: Harper and Brothers, 1940. A useful study of Wilde and his works in relation to the last decade of the 1890s.

Index

(The works of Wilde are listed under his name)

172